LEADERSHIP GIRL

Empowering Women Entrepreneurs to Achieve Extraordinary Results by Capturing Massive Sales

AUTHOR:

Haley Lynn Gray

EDITOR:

Susan McGuire

Published by Best Seller Publishing®, Pasadena, CA
Best Seller Publishing® is a registered trademark
Printed in the United States of America.

ISBN-13:978-1523270934
ISBN-10:1523270934

This publication is designed to provide accurate and authoritative information with regard to the subject matter covered. It is sold with the understanding that the publisher is not engaged in rendering legal, accounting, or other professional advice. If legal advice or other expert assistance is required, the services of a competent professional should be sought. The opinions expressed by the authors in this book are not endorsed by Best Seller Publishing® and are the sole responsibility of the author rendering the opinion.

Most Best Seller Publishing® titles are available at special quantity discounts for bulk purchases for sales promotions, premiums, fundraising, and educational use. Special versions or book excerpts can also be created to fi t specifi c needs.

For more information, please write:
Best Seller Publishing®
1346 Walnut Street, #205
Pasadena, CA 91106
or call 1(626) 765 9750
Toll Free: 1(844) 850-3500
Visit us online at: www.BestSellerPublishing.org

This book is dedicated to my father, Claude Wilson. He had the confidence that I could set out and do anything I wanted to, so I did.

TABLE OF CONTENTS

Time Management, Priorities & Goals

Leadership

Closing

INTRODUCTION

Why Did I Write This Book?

I wrote this book because I wanted to share the lessons I learned from starting my own businesses and while getting my MBA from Duke University. I started **Leadership Girl** while I was atttending Duke University, where I eventually graduated with my Masters of Business Administration (MBA) and a concentration in Entrepreneurship and Innovation.

As a multi-passionate entrepreneur and owner of several successful businesses, I enjoy helping people build their own prosperous businesses, and I want to support them in their hopes and dreams. Helping someone build a business enables them to send their child to dance lessons or cub scouts, and... they won't be pouring money into the deep pockets of a large corporation.

It surprised me to see that only 10% of my Weekend Executive MBA class was women. And in my previous job, when I'd go into meetings with a group of managers - sometimes as many as 20-30 people in the meeting - I would be the only woman in the room. It seemed odd to me that women really aren't participating in leadership or entrepreneurship at nearly the same rate as their male counterparts.

I also came across a Forbes Article which shows the huge disparity in the number of women who are entrepreneurs to men.[1] Because entrepreneurship and being a business owner typically allow more flexibility and options for how you choose to spend your time, it seemed odd to me that more women aren't entrepreneurs.

---

[1]   http://www.forbes.com/sites/babson/2012/12/05/closing-the-gender-gap-for-women-entrepreneurs/

During my studies, I realized that most of the growth in the economy comes from small to medium size businesses. Large businesses are aggregators of jobs. So, if we want to see sustained improvement in the economy, and more jobs, we need to foster entrepreneurs, and enable them to be successful. Helping small to medium sized businesses has become a mission of mine since I started Leadership Girl.

I've been coaching business owners since 2011, and helping them make their business dreams a reality - people like you. Throughout the time I was studying for my MBA, I was often approached by people who asked lots of questions about business, and who asked for my help.

I founded and own a home care agency named **Extension of You Home Care**, I own a **Care Patrol** Franchise, and I am also the driving force behind **LeadershipGirl.com**. I eat my own dog food. If I'm telling you to try something in your business, I've tried it and found it to work. I'll be happy to also tell you what I have found that doesn't work. That's how I roll: helping people build successful businesses through the benefits of my education and my experience.

I'm a best-selling author, and released my first book last year: "Choosing a Caregiver". I have also contributed to Duke's Weekend Executive MBA Blog, as well as a number of other online resources. I have two blogs of my own: LeadershipGirl.com, which is the basis of this book, and TheExtensionofYou.com, which is the blog for my Home Care agency. I guess you could say I have a lot of words to get out.

Though my businesses are successful, I have made my fair share of mistakes, and learned some things the hard way. Since I've learned those lessons the hard way, I'm able to help you avoid making similar mistakes!

Have a seat, and pull out a highlighter to mark up your favorite parts, or get your notepad and take notes. In this book, you'll find the best entrepreneur information we've got, compiled together for your enjoyment. It is intended to be used as a reference guide, so you don't have to read everything all at once. You can jump around between chapters and pick and choose what you want to read. I try to present information in bite-size pieces; I hope you'll find it useful.

http://www.forbes.com/sites/babson/2012/12/05/closing-the-gender-gap-for-women-entrepreneurs/

THE INS & OUTS OF ENTREPRENEURSHIP

Facing Job Loss

Most people will face a job loss at some point in their careers. It used to be that those people were tarnished with the brush, and people wondered if they sucked, what they did wrong, and whether they were just plain losers. Things have changed a lot since then. It's really no longer the case that people who have been laid off are seen in a negative light. Layoffs, restructuring and re-organization in a business or corporation have become incredibly commonplace. Regardless of that fact, people who lose their jobs frequently experience a lot of negative feelings, including depression, despair and anxiety. I know because I've been one of those people. I've had a lot of friends who have also faced job loss, and it is not easy for them.

I was first laid off from IBM in 2005, as part of a large layoff with 1200 other people. It didn't take long for me to find a job because I spent close to 60 hours per week job seeking. My resume was also mostly up to date, so I didn't have to spend a month crafting a new resume. That meant applying for jobs, updating my resume for each job, and networking. In 2006, when I was pregnant with my fourth child, I was laid off again. This time, it was because the entire branch office closed down. Frankly, I had some really hard decisions to make, including whether I even wanted to go back to work. My life had gotten really busy: I was pregnant with my fourth child, I was managing a full house, and managing my parents' care needs at the same time. Ultimately, I decided to accept another full time position, where I stayed for 7 years.

Getting laid off and losing your job is a bit like losing part of your identity. You also worry that you're going to lose friends, and that you're going to be a social pariah. In some ways, it's like dealing with the death of a loved one. Truthfully, that does happen to some extent, because people don't know what to say, so they don't say anything at all. Some people may avoid you entirely. So, you may lose some friends. On the other hand, there will be others who will appear, and show themselves to be true friends. They will be your best advocates.

It's okay to cry, and mope, and give yourself time to grieve. Grief, shock, anger, and all sorts of emotions are a normal part of the process, and they shouldn't be ignored. In fact, I think that ignoring the changes and the grief makes the situation even more stressful.

So, what can you do? Acknowledge the loss, grief, anger, and other feelings you're having as completely normal. Give yourself some time - a few days to a week. But set a limit.

Then pick up that resume and dust it off. Start customizing your resume to suit the different positions for which you're applying. Understand that all of the activities of finding a new job are your new job. Treat them as such. Make them important. Also, make sure that your friends, family and network know that you're looking for a job. Open positions are often found through someone you know. Be sure to use your connections.

Waiting until you've lost your job is not necessarily the best way to start networking though, so if you can, start building your network before you are laid off.

Know that this phase shall pass, and that you will emerge from the other side. You will be a changed person, and that is not a bad thing. I found that losing my job gave me clarity on what I wanted to do, and where I wanted to go.

Losing a job is a blessing to many people, even if they don't see it that way at the time. It is an opportunity to craft your next career, and tackle those goals that you've had for a while. Change can be good. You get to decide how you react and respond to it. Will it be a good change or a negative one?

What about you? Have you been through a job loss? How did you react? What did you do?

Why I Became an Entrepreneur

Most people who start a business have a reason for doing so, and I'm no different. I didn't set out to start my own businesses because I thought that it would be easier than working a normal, corporate job, but rather because I felt a calling and a bit of the need to change the world for each of the businesses that I own now.

This is my story...

My parents moved to the Raleigh area in 2005, wanting to be closer to family, and specifically to be closer to their grandchildren. What I discovered when they moved up here is that neither one of them was doing terribly well, and that we had to start providing help to them nearly from the day that they moved up here and bought a lovely 3200 square foot home. Because, you know, they needed that huge house to hold all of their stuff, and to rattle around in. They needed a lot of help getting their stuff moved, organized, hung, and where they wanted it in the house. That was just the first step though.

Since Mom had Multiple Sclerosis (MS), Dad was her full-time caregiver. She couldn't or wouldn't cook, or prepare any of her meals. So she was fully dependent on Dad to prepare her food, just so - half of a peanut butter and jelly sandwich with half a plate of cut up fruit for lunches, a salad for dinner, and a small entrée. Almost everything about her was fairly high maintenance, and he was in charge of it.

Only - Dad's health was declining. We noticed fairly quickly after they moved, that Dad was having trouble with some tasks, like writing and following complex conversations. He also complained a lot about back pain. We knew that he had arthritis, but what we didn't fully appreciate was the severity of his osteoporosis, and how quickly his back was fracturing

- and we didn't understand or appreciate the severity of the problem until after 2011 - years later. We took him to various doctors, orthopedists, a neurologist, a neurosurgeon, and another neurologist, neurosurgeon, and around and around. He was tested multiple times, wound up in the hospital, and was quickly discharged, with home health care. Of course, we had no warning each time. The hospital and social workers just waved their hands, and told us that home health care would come by, and take care of them, and everything would be okay.

The lesson I learned from this ordeal was that everything wasn't just going to be okay, and that there were assumptions on the part of the social workers that I was fully available to take care of my parents. That wasn't the case at all. I had four young children who needed their mother. I also had a full time job, and trying to stay employed and further my career during that time. To say that it was hard would be an understatement. There were days that I was literally in tears trying to balance it all, and the assumption that I could do more, was frustrating almost beyond description.

We hired private duty home care for my parents at various intervals, and they would quickly let the caregivers go because they didn't want to spend the money. See, people are conditioned in the United States to think that all care is covered by insurance, and if it isn't, then you must not need whatever that care is. That is the reality with home care. It's not paid for by Medicare, so my parents thought that they didn't need it.

Mom and Dad needed the help, but didn't want to admit it. They eventually agreed to have someone come in to prepare meals, and do some light chores for them, but not to have someone there all the time. It nearly took an act of congress to get them to keep a caregiver.

Let me tell you the story about the time my mom had to go to urgent care because she was having trouble breathing. They left the caregiver at home to let the maid in. Dad drove Mom to the urgent care, where they promptly took one look at her and told her that she needed to be transported to the hospital. My dad called me at work (imagine the screaming going through my head) to ask me to meet him at home, and then drive my mom to the emergency room. Since the hospital was in the next town over, they needed me to take care of it, when they had perfectly competent help who could have driven them to the hospital. Mom spent over a week in the hospital for congestive heart failure, pneumonia and flu. Then another 4 weeks in rehab, before being booted out for failing to eat. Actually, she didn't like the food, so she refused to eat anything they served. And she certainly wasn't going to drink thickened liquids, and my parents wouldn't sign a waiver. So, her weight dropped to 85 pounds before she was sent home with 24-hour caregivers. The caregiver lasted about six weeks before my parents decided they hated the loss of privacy.

I fought them every time they decided to let their caregivers go, but since they were adults, they had the right to choose whether to receive care or not. My dad's perspective was that he hated spending the money, and wanted me to "just drop by" for a few minutes here and there to help do things. I had to explain that I had a full time job, four very young children, and couldn't just drop everything every time that they needed a bit of help with chores around the house. They knew that they needed help with meal preparation, grocery shopping, laundry, housekeeping, changing litter boxes, and more. They flat-out refused to pay for any kind of help until I put my foot down and insisted that they had to hire someone because I really could not do everything they needed done, nor could I meet all of their needs.

Eventually Dad's health declined enough that he had to have a caregiver around the clock. It was at that point that my eyes were truly opened to the home care industry. I got to see the good, the bad and the really ugly sides of the home care business. It was then that I felt the need to change how things are done. By starting my own home care agency.

I got so many nudges along the way. Things like my dad being left unattended by a caregiver. A caregiver who never once, in two years of working as his caregiver, saw a supervisor during her shift, caregivers that poured kitty litter on top of the poop, and the crowning glory - the caregiver who gave him alcohol. There were so many things I could see that needed changing, and are actually industry best practices, but so few people follow them.

I interviewed lots of caregivers and found their pain points. As it turned out, almost all of my dad's good caregivers work for me now, because they are so passionate about providing exemplary care, and providing amazing care is what we do for our clients. And we take good care of the caregivers too.

I decided I was going to start a business with solid foundations and good business principles, a business that takes good care of both employees and clients. So that is what I've done. Over the last two years, I've slowly and methodically built what I believe is the best home care agency in my area. We take the best possible care of our clients - the way that they want to be taken care of, and to their standards.

What's Your Reason?

It has been my experience that most people who start a business or volunteer a lot of hours for an organization do it for a reason. There is some driving force for them, which nudges them to step out and start a business, and go through all of the work that it entails. For me, I am a multi-passionate entrepreneur, and I'm also a Girl Scout leader. In each case, I have found that my reason for getting involved in these activities has been to make a difference in people's lives. How I got there in each case is a different story.

Extension of You Home Care

Senior Home Care is one of those industries that has a very mixed reputation. There are some exceptional providers out there, and there are some rather dubious players as well. I got to see the good, bad and ugly of the industry when I was taking care of my parents. Since my mom had Multiple Sclerosis (MS), and my Dad had Parkinson's, I had plenty of opportunities, over the course of almost 6 years, to observe various home care agencies up close and personal. As a result of those experiences, I decided to drive change in the industry, and I am now the founder and CEO of Extension of You Home Care. It is something that I felt compelled to do, and I can't say that I regret it at all. We are making a difference in the lives of our clients and our caregivers every day.

Girl Scout Leader

All too often, girls are told to sit down, shut up, and be good girls. As I was growing up, there was certainly the expectation that girls would be silent and not heard. When the opportunity arose for me to help out with my oldest daughter's Daisy troop in Kindergarten, I reluctantly entered into the fray, deciding that I'd do it for perhaps a year or two, because I knew what a great experience I had in Brownies growing up, and how many opportunities I had as a result.

Fast forward a few years - my oldest Girl Scouts have graduated from high school, and I'm still a Girl Scout leader. I've had the opportunity to work with girls, and learn a lot of really cool business skills through the Girl Scout Cookie program. We've had a large number of girls earn their Girl Scout Bronze, Silver, and Gold Awards, which are the three highest awards that a girl can earn in Girl Scouts.

The leadership opportunities, as well as the challenges that we put in front of the girls to grow and stretch, are extraordinary. We are encouraging the girls to sit up, roar, and show the world what they can do. We grow them into leaders and influencers.

Leadership Girl

When I was attending Duke University, 10% of my class was women. At my previous place of employment, when I'd attend meetings with about 20 managers and senior technical personnel, I was frequently the only woman there. This got me curious, so I started doing some digging. I found that women make up about 50% of the population. Yet, we only make up 5% of entrepreneurs. Why is that? I see women jumping into selling all sorts of things, like make-up, housewares and various other items. They spend many hours of their lives peddling these items, yet they never seem to achieve financial independence. To me, those facts are alarming. I see it often though. From my research, I've learned that true financial independence comes from being an entrepreneur and leader. Having a job and being paid by someone else isn't going to give women the flexibility that they need to comfortably raise their families, and it also isn't going to give them the income that they need. I recognized a skill gap, and I've been working on educating women, and supporting and empowering them to become entrepreneurs and leaders in their industries. That's why I created Leadership Girl. To make a difference in the lives of women, and men.

My Reason

I have started to realize that my reason and purpose for being here is to enable people to achieve their best, to get what they need. Everything that I'm involved in is focused on enabling that purpose. I think it is who I am at a cellular level, and I'm enjoying being able to follow that mission and reason.

What about you? What are your reasons? What is your mission? Have you found your mission yet?

Do What You Love

I've heard it said over and over again that if you do what you love, it will seem right, and that you'll do better in your career. I think that it's important to note that you are going to spend a large percentage of your waking hours working. If that career or work is something that makes you miserable, the quality of your life is going to be very different than if you are doing something you love. One of the reasons I started my companies is that I started focusing on what I like to do, and what I'm good at. I also started thinking about what I don't like doing. Of course, I also found some interesting opportunities that I realized were available, and seized on those. I think that focusing on what it is that makes your heart sing and your soul hum is important.

I realized there were a lot of things I was doing in my previous career that I didn't love, and wasn't particularly good at. It took me years to accept that I was on a path that wasn't feeding my soul, and making me happy, despite earning a very good income.

After the deaths of both of my parents, and both of my husband's parents, I realized that life really can be too short, and that to spend the time I have remaining on this earth in a job that I didn't particularly love, and wasn't totally thrilled about (and honestly, I don't think that they were really in love with me either), was not a good choice.

I had to really look into the mirror to see what I saw reflected. By digging deep in my soul, I found that I really had a passion for helping others, and that I wanted to change my entire lifestyle. Going from a corporate job to starting my own companies was certainly a shock to the system. It wasn't easy, but it has been tremendously rewarding.

Do you do what you love?

Entrepreneurship is hard work, and frequently involves many long hours. It is not unusual for me to spend 16-20 hours per day working. The upside is that I'm able to work when it is convenient for my family, and to move my working schedule around their needs. Frankly, if I didn't like what I was doing, it would be rather miserable. But I like what I'm doing. That's true even if my daughter says I don't have a "real" job. I recognize that I'm making a difference in people's lives with the work that we are doing at Extension of You Home Care, Leadership Girl, and Care Patrol. We run our business the way that we believe is the right way: by treating people the way that they want, and deserve, to be treated. We follow through on our promises, and follow up to see how the client is doing. The way it should be. And it makes me happy.

Entrepreneurship involves hours and hours of work, and a good amount of sweat and tears. But, it's worth it, and it's something that I love. It is making a difference in people's lives every day.

What about you? Have you created a life and career for yourself that you love?

How Female Entrepreneurs are Different

People who get out there and make their own business from scratch are called Entrepreneurs and they can be male or female. However, male and female entrepreneurs do things very differently when it comes time to running a business. There are significant differences in the demands that society puts on the genders. Those differences and demands will affect how women and men treat their jobs, because their needs are distinctly different in some ways.

Female entrepreneurs tend to be more sensitive to her clients' and employees' needs than a male entrepreneur will tend to be. Female entrepreneurs want to make sure their employees are taken care of so there won't be a high turn-over rate. Not only do they want to take care of their workers, but they will also ensure their clients are satisfied and happy with the service they are receiving. Client satisfaction matters to female entrepreneurs because they don't want to lose clients from poor service.

Not only will female entrepreneurs make sure their clients and employees are pleased, but they tend to be hard workers because they feel they have to prove they can do the job just as good, or better, than a male can do it. They feel they have to prove they are capable of the work and handling the business they are in.

Female entrepreneurs are generally more serious, more likely to seek and listen to advice, and better at dealing with people than most male entrepreneurs are.

Female entrepreneurs will often have to juggle work with family demands on their time. It doesn't mean that their job is any less important. It just means that in many families, there is an expectation that the female will be the one to cook dinner, clean the house, and deal with kid issues, and much more.

Male entrepreneurs are more interested in the growth of the business and the money side of things because they want to make lots of money, and make it quick. Men are more interested in the business side of their business rather than the people side. They have much less interest in being there for their employees who help run the business. They will also be very interested in getting new clients. However, they will not take as good care of these clients as females will.

Both men and women have strengths and weakness when it comes to running a business, however, they both are capable of doing the job and getting it done right. Women more than men tend to be there for their employees and clients. And men tend to want to make more money and worry less about their employees' happiness. Both men and women have to build off of their strengths and learn from their weakness to make the business last for a long time to come.

One strength women have is their desire to talk and deal with people. But they often need more help on the business and money side of things, so they are more willing to ask for advice. This does not make them bad entrepreneurs; however, it makes them very good at what they do.

By being aware of the differences between men and women, and the fact that individuals have different strengths and weaknesses, we can build the best companies and businesses. It's important to note that not everyone within the same gender has the same strengths and weaknesses, so you do have to be a bit careful with generalizations.

Moms Re-Entering the Work Force

If you have taken time off to have kids, chances are you thought that reentering the workforce would be easy when the time came.

However, many women are finding that stepping out to take care of children has a significantly negative impact on their careers. It can be far harder to find a job, and even when they do find a job, they usually have to take a huge step backwards, sometimes even starting over again in their careers, if they can even get hired in the first place. I have talked to countless women about the challenge of getting back into the workforce after a prolonged absence. All too often they are unable to find a job in the industry they worked in before, and this is particularly true of the technology sector. If you've been out of tech for more than 18 months, you are going to have to start your career over again.

Adding to the challenge, many women still have relatively young children when they are re-entering the workforce, so they need to ensure that they still retain flexibility in scheduling, because chances are, getting back into the job market means that they are going to be earning less than their spouse who has continued to work. Now, this is a two-way street - if a man stays home with his children, he faces the same hurdles, but most of the parents who elect to stay at home with kids when they're little are women.

So, what's a parent to do?

There are so many Multilevel Marketing (MLM) schemes out there that it can practically make your head spin. The problem is, unless you are absolutely fantastic with sales, and you are willing to put a gazillion hours into it, and recruit the heck out of getting people to be your down-line, you're not really going to make any money at it. I think that for most people, MLM's are not the best way to go because you're just putting money back into a large corporation' pockets.

Another real option is to start your own business, using skills you likely had while working in corporate America and while managing a growing household.

Truth is, many of the skills you already have can be applied to small business ownership. Multi-tasking, customer service, bookkeeping, team or household management, and computer skills - these all translate just fine. You can craft a career that may be demanding, but it will accommodate your family and your family's needs. If you need to take time off to take your child to the doctor, you're not exactly going to get a 'talking to' from the boss. You will end up having to make that time up later, once the kids are in bed though. You get to choose how you're going to spend your time.

Being your own boss puts you in the driver's seat and allows you to make money on your own terms. You can put as much or as little time into it as you need (within reason), and your results will correspond the same way. Being an entrepreneur can be a fantastic option for moms who want to make some money and get back into the job market. They certainly aren't going to face any discrimination while doing it, either. That's because people have a huge amount of respect for entrepreneurs.

Now, how will you start your business? How will you make it a success?

Proven Tips for Working from Home… With Children

When women have their first child, they often want the best of both worlds – stay home with baby, and be able to contribute financially to the family – while working from home. This sounds like the ideal situation… that is, until you actually try to do the work with children present. If you don't set a realistic tone for your work-at-home venture early on, this will turn into frustration fast. Children are lovely distractions, and they want lots of attention, but if you use some simple tricks; you'll stand a better chance of getting stuff done.

Here are 4 Tips to Actually Get Stuff Done

1. **SET REASONABLE DEADLINES.** Since you're working from home, all or most of your work will be done online, which is super convenient. Make sure to choose the best schedules and deadlines that work with your family's (read: your children's) lives. Always build in a buffer for getting projects done when possible, in case of last minute emergencies, like sick children or snow days.

2. **BUY "WORK ONLY" TOYS.** Depending on the age of your children (obviously outside of infancy), your children will understand the concept of special time and special toys. Buy them special toys for when you're working. Only pull the special "work toys" out when you're working and be sure they never play with them during non-work hours. Buy quiet toys, books, and educational tablets that will give you some uninterrupted time for calls and last minute projects.

3. **HIRE A BABYSITTER.** Children of a certain age may not be willing to leave you alone, no matter how many new toys you buy, or which TV shows you put them in front of. That is the point where you may need to hire a babysitter, to watch them. Be sure you clearly and carefully

explain that you need to focus on getting work done. By eliminating distractions, you'll be able to focus on getting more work done in a shorter period of time, and that will give you more time to spend with your family. Cut yourself some slack if you need to hire outside help. Sometimes it really does take a village to raise a child.

4. **SET REALISTIC EXPECTATIONS.** Even though you are working from home, it's important to lay some ground rules for your family so they take your business seriously. Explain to everyone that your work is just as important as a job outside the home, that it's important to you and to the family as a whole, and that you're going to need a realistic amount of time alone to get your work done and be productive.

To help young children learn appropriate behaviors for when Mommy is working, set up a reward system. For the first couple of weeks, praise the correct behaviors so they understand what you expect and where your boundaries are.

Help your spouse or significant other understand that you are going to be working during certain hours, and are thus unavailable to do household chores, run errands, or otherwise handle certain tasks. This is critical, because setting those expectations up front will save you a lot of frustration in the long run. My husband was fairly certain I was sitting at home eating bon-bons and playing on Facebook all day, until he stayed home a few days, and got to see what I was really doing. Setting his expectation levels were probably the hardest, as he could see the drop in my income when I left my regular job, and the lack of income coming in the early days of my business.

Working from home is absolutely doable. The important thing is to stick to a routine as much as possible, set boundaries and expectations from the beginning, and don't forget that your family is the reason you do this. Flexibility and understanding is key to successfully working from home.

Bodacious Ideas for Passive Income Streams

Looking for passive income ideas? People often think that making money is incredibly hard to do. I think that it requires a shift in mindset, and some ingenuity.

Really, you have to create something, or sell something that someone else would like to buy. There are so many ways that you can do that, and one of the simplest is to create a website, and sell a product that people are willing to spend their money on. It really is that simple. Create a service or business that others want to pay for. It can be quite simple, or utterly elaborate.

Look at ways to solve problems for your clients, and address their pain points.

Here are 9 Passive Income ideas to get your creative juices flowing:

1. **THE WEEKLY FAMILY MEAL PLANNER AND GROCERY LIST.** You can make a list of recipes, and include the shopping list, which will allow people to shop for their groceries, and have their entire weekly meals planned out. People really like to not have to think out what they're going to eat. Anything you can do to simplify meal planning will make your client's quality of life improve.

2. **MONTHLY COOK/FREEZE RECIPES** for the crock-pot, including a grocery list, so that all of a family's meal preparation is done for the month in one day, except for dropping a bag from the freezer into the crock-pot each day.

3. Develop a **MONTHLY EXERCISE PLAN**, with diagrams, checklists and videos.

4. Develop an **EYE MAKE-UP TUTORIAL**, for various kinds of eye make-up. Show how to obtain different looks with different tools. Include photos, videos and stencils for obtaining this result. Other options could be eyebrows, cheeks, or skin care.

5. Monthly **MAINTENANCE CHECKLIST FOR YOUR HOME**, and show how to do each piece of maintenance with a video.

6. **PHOTOGRAPHY COURSES**, with a checklist and ideas for how to do things. This is especially helpful if the information is written out with lots of illustrations and examples. Videos help too.

7. **SOFTWARE COURSES** that teach how to use various types of software, like Adobe.

8. **PARTY IN A BOX** – Pick a birthday party theme, and include instructions for how to make each of the decorations, with videos, and lots of beautiful pictures.

9. Develop a **HOW-TO COURSE FOR LINKEDIN** that shows someone how to get started, find contacts, and how to use it for business purposes to find employees, market your business, and find your ideal client.

I could go on and on here, but the only real limit is your imagination. You truly can build so many different products, market them, and make a decent income from them. Truly, the best thing you can do is go ahead and build your product offerings, and start trying them out on your test market to see how they do. That will help you get offerings out there, and start building an income stream.

Things Successful People DO

I've been looking at my life over the last year or so, and thinking about what specifically sets successful people apart from others. My life has changed dramatically in the last 5 years, and it accelerated dramatically about 2 years ago when I changed careers. I started wondering, "What do successful people do differently from people who are less successful? What is it about those things that they do that makes them successful?"

6 Things Successful People Do

1. **SET REALISTIC, ACHIEVABLE AND AGGRESSIVE GOALS** – Seriously, if you're not going to do anything else, you have to do this. You're not going to go anywhere if you don't have any idea of what it is you want to do. Not all outcomes are created equally, and while you can float along in life, it will only take you so far. Most people who are successful set hourly, daily, weekly, monthly, and yearly goals. It's a game to see if they can meet those goals.

2. **STICK WITH IT** – The things that are most worth having are worth working on. But that means sticking with them. Persistence pays off. It can be hard to stick with things when the shit hits the fan, but that is likely precisely when you need to stick with it. Persistence is critical in business and career success. I've said before: success in business is about 5% inspiration, and the rest is perspiration and perseverence.

3. **MAKE CONTINUOUS IMPROVEMENTS** – Things rarely work out perfectly the first time, so the key is to make continuous improvements over a longer period of time. Every time you do something, stop and analyze how you did on it. Then figure out what you need to change to do it better. I'm sure you'll find many ways to improve. You can

then focus on making those changes and seeing how they impact the outcome.

4. **Don't strive for perfection** – You don't have to do things perfectly the first time. In fact, if you stop and wait until everything is perfect, you will paralyze yourself, and you'll never make any progress. Some women I talk to want to launch their business, but they won't do anything until the website is perfect, the copy is perfect, they've built their email list, and their offerings are perfectly figured out. The reality of business is that you'll try to make as many plans as possible, and only about thalf of those will work out. You might as well accept that, and act in that vein.

5. **Know When to Fight** – It is worth knowing when to fight, and when to just ignore something. Just because you aren't arguing with someone doesn't mean that you are agreeing with him or her. It just means that you're not wasting your breath arguing with them. Let's face it, not everyone is going to like you or respect you. Arguing with them isn't going to change that. Save your breath and energy, and focus on positive things. This is so important. Some people want to create drama just because they are drama llamas. Ignore them and let them go. They may be clients, employees, family members, or any other peole in your life. Don't feed the llamas; just let them loose.

6. **Let Little Things Go** – Sometimes you have to decide when to let something go, and concentrate your energy on the big picture. For me, that happens in a variety of ways. I have gotten help with the yard, for instance. That means that I don't have to focus on pulling weeds and mowing grass. I can focus my energy on spending time doing the things that have a bigger impact and make more of a difference.

   You are going to eventually have to give up control over every single facet of your business. The sooner you accept that things will be imperfect, and that you can relinquish control over certain things, the happier you will be. Get help with your email calendar and email. Find someone who can make phone calls for you. Delegate, and let it go.

The key here is focusing your energy on what is important. Figure out which steps you personally need to follow to ensure your success. That will require actually doing something towards those goals. You can't just think about your goals and hope and pray that they come true. You must take concrete action to make them come into being. You also have to deal with the fact that there are only 24 hours in a day, and you only go so far. There is only one you. Make the time that you do spend worth it.

Things Successful People DON'T Do

When I wrote <u>Things that Successful People Do</u>. I realized that there are just as many things that successful people don't do. Or rather, things that successful people do to overcome challenges.

Things Successful People Don't Do

1. **THEY DON'T ALLOW NEGATIVE THOUGHTS TO TAKE OVER THEIR MINDS.** That is not to say that they should be unrealistic, but I've found that successful people generally do focus on the positive, rather than on the negative. And they don't talk bad TO themselves. If you see yourself as bad, dumb, stupid, or whatever, then you project that image. I frequently laugh, because I am a fat lady, and I think that a lot of times people don't realize it, or they don't realize just HOW fat I am because I don't project that image. It comes across in so many ways, but it does get to be downright comical at times. Yes, I know I need to lose weight, and I work on it constantly. But I don't beat myself up for it either. It is what it is, and it is changing, and I don't allow it to rule my life.

   If you stop and stew about things, and think bad thoughts constantly, then that will become your reality. It is true. The more negativity you open the door to, and invite into your life, the more that negativity will rule you. You can decide how you interpret each situation you encounter. Is it positive, neutral, or negative? Can you laugh about the fact that an employee locked the car door with the keys inside the car with it still running? Or are you going to get upset about it?

2. **THEY DON'T ALLOW EXCUSES TO GET IN THEIR WAY.** How many times have you heard someone say that they'll do something once they lose weight, or that they'll do something once the number of

hits on their webpage gets to where they want, or wait to publish a book because the bounce rate on their website is too high? Seriously. I think that sometimes we are our own worst enemies here. Between the negative talk and excuses, how do people get any work done? Simply? They don't allow them to. Just set a goal and go for it.

Live your life with no excuses. It's OK to not be right 100% of the time. You are going to have to deal with the fact that there will always be competition out there, and some of it will be better than you. Where you will win is in having a positive, can-do attitude, and not making any excuses. Like the Nike brand - "Just do it". Or take a note from Yoda, "Do or Do Not, there is no try."

3. **ALLOW ANALYSIS PARALYSIS TAKE OVER** – One of the worst things you can do is to allow analysis paralysis to take over. Sure, there will always be a better way to do something. But, if you spend too much time trying to figure out which way to do something, you can really cost yourself in time and money. Sometimes a good enough answer is going to be fine. Will it be perfect? Nope. But, the decision is likely to be serviceable, and allow you to move on with your life. Take that as being good enough.

   I've spent a lot of time educating employees that the 80% solution is truly adequate in many cases. Could we do better? Perhaps. But if the cost doesn't justify the result, then we need to think twice about it. That is not to say that there are certain situations where 100% is the only acceptable answer. One example of this is drug screens for employees. The drug screens come back either positive or negative. There isn't anything in between. As the saying goes, 'You can't be a little bit pregnant'. But, if you're writing a blog post, it may be that the solution which is good, is good enough.

4. **BURN BRIDGES** – Remember that the world is an incredibly small place. If you burn bridges and annoy people, it will come back to you. Karma is a bitch. And be careful about stabbing people in the back, or setting them up for failure. You could be setting yourself up for a later act of revenge or Karma. Just don't go there. It's not worth it. You'll give yourself a lousy reputation. Learning when to shut your mouth is a priceless lesson.

It is true that sometimes you can't keep your mouth shut. Make those cases few and far between, and worth having the fight come back onto you. I pick my battles very carefully, and in most cases would choose to not burn a bridge. If it's a former employer, former employee, or other similar case, I don't burn a bridge unless I have no other choice.

5. LIE – Mean what you say, and say what you mean. Don't lie. It never goes over well. You may get away with it for a while, but eventually, you will be found out, and you will destroy your reputation. Once you've done that, it's nearly impossible to get back. It's easier to start good, and stay that way. So, just tell the truth, and it will go much better for you.

In general, I think that negative energy begets more negative energy, so you have to be very careful with it. I'm not saying that you should always turn the other cheek or let people steamroller you. What I'm saying is that you should selectively stand up for yourself, when it makes sense to do so. There are many times that we get caught up in the emotions of situations, and retaliation, that cost us exponentially in the future, through destroyed relationships and worsened reputations.

Use Project-Based Freelancers More Efficiently as an Entrepreneur

Every day of the month for an entrepreneur means one thing. It means our business needs our attention – invoices to send, sales calls to make, a blog to update – and how are you going to get it all done?

Well, you will, but likely not as well as you'd like to, and definitely not as quickly as could happen.

You knew going in that owning your own business is a lot of work, so hard work is not something that entrepreneurs, like yourself, mind doing. The problem with owning your own business, however, is that you can't be great at absolutely every part of business, no matter your degree equivalent. You may be an excellent graphic artist, but you may know nothing about how to balance your books.

To compete with other small businesses in your same niche or market, you're going to have to get help at some point. Learning to delegate effectively and hire freelancers to help with your projects will help your business now and in the future.

Here are my 4 best ways to delegate more efficiently as an entrepreneur:

1. **FIGURE OUT YOUR NEEDS.** What's been holding your small business back? Are there areas that need the most attention: marketing, computer work, social media, something else? If you have a mentor or coach, ask her for advice on how to grow in these particular areas of your business. She will be able to point you in the right direction to find the best freelancers to help your business as well. If you don't already have an experienced entrepreneur or businessperson helping

you, you should find one. A great reference is SCORE. SCORE is a nonprofit that provides counseling for small businesses. Also, be sure to take time to define the project and its scope distinctly, then schedule the project before you look for someone to help you complete it.

2. **APPRAISE YOUR BUSINESS AND PROFESSIONAL STRENGTHS.** The amount and type of assistance you'll need depends on your abilities, weaknesses and areas that you want to strengthen further in your business or professional life. There are freelancers available in many different areas, such as blog writing, tax preparation and public relations. The type of assistance you need depends on your abilities, your weaknesses and areas you want to strengthen in your business. Using a freelancer (or many freelancers) will allow you to focus on what you personally do best in your business, whether it's writing blogs, selling, or coaching.

3. **START YOUR FREELANCER SEARCH.** Where can you find good freelancers? There are huge freelancing companies, such as Elance, Guru and oDesk that have tens of thousands of freelancers from across the world. Moving through these huge websites of freelancers seems like more work; they are complicated and only add to work that you already have to do. Depending on the site, you may have to pay an escrow, there are bidding wars, it can be difficult to find a freelancer with the skills you're looking for in the country you'd like, and you may have troubles finding one within your price range. Plus, the number of resumes to read can be overwhelming. Take your time and find the one freelancer you're looking for. If it doesn't work with one, move on to the next. There are hundreds who are looking for jobs; no need to waste time with a freelancer who continually makes mistakes. Depending on the type of freelancer you need, you may want to look for niche freelance companies that screen their candidates and require them to invest some time into the screening process. The niche sites have far fewer members. You'll only have to review 10 resumes instead of over 100 applicants. This may lower your possibilities of success in finding the perfect freelancer, but it can also significantly cut the amount of time you invest in this process. To find the right niche freelancer website, just search for the specific work you need, followed by the word freelancer. For example, if you need graphics

done for your Facebook page, search for "graphic design freelancer". The worst mistake that first time employers make is to hire based on the freelancer price alone. The most inexpensive freelancer is likely to have zero experience in your niche or field. This isn't a bargain price if you're spending hours of your time training them to do work that isn't up to par, or that could have been done in a quarter of the time by someone who charges only double the amount. Review freelancer samples and portfolios (if available) before offering a contract. Be sure to ask for all references that were done during freelancing (not during out-of-the-home work time). Ask questions and have a phone or Skype interview to schedule and invite the freelancer's input on the project at hand.

4. **GET STARTED.** Any good relationship begins with respect, and this is especially true of a client/freelancer relationship. If your freelancer promised projects with a 48-hour turnaround time, be sure that you communicate these expectations and that they reciprocate with the project on time or beforehand. If your freelancer is an especially long distance away, be sure to review her work in 2-3 stages throughout the project so you're up to date on the progress of your project. If your freelancer does a particularly great job, or completes the project ahead of schedule, be prepared to pay an extra bonus to keep her around. Once you find the right freelancer, you'll want to make more projects for her to save yourself time for other business priorities and do what YOU do best.

What have you found that have been the best ways to use your freelancer? How many hours do you think you've saved in your business?

Painful Lessons in Entrepreneurship

I've been in business long enough to have made some pretty spectacular mistakes. Every entrepreneur makes mistakes, and it is the mark of a good entrepreneur when they can look back on the things that they've done, and identify what things went well, and why those things went well. It's also important to understand what didn't go so well, and what the reason for the failure was.

I've also gotten some things very right.

Here Are 3 of My Most Painful Lessons in Entrepreneurship:

1. **NOT GETTING AN OFFICE EARLIER ON.** We have a team that is all over the area. Office papers were located in no less than 4 different locations. That meant that when we needed to find things, sometimes it was impossible. In fact, now that we have an office, we are still finding things that are missing or misplaced. We lost tremendous amounts of productivity due to being distributed across multiple locations. The other downside is that we had printed materials in all of those locations. When we got all the office stuff together, we found that we had piles and piles of printed materials, which amounted to hundreds of dollars in printed materials, and wasted money.

    LESSON LEARNED: Get an office in the early stages, and you can hold people accountable. Working from home sounds lovely. If you're a boss, it's not so great, because in practice it gets abused. I saw ample evidence of employees claiming they were being super productive, but when I looked at what they actually accomplished, it was nowhere near what it should have been. Paperwork will be much easier to sort and organize because it will all be located in one place.

2. **FAILING TO GET AN ADVISOR.** Too often in business, your employees are going to tell you "yes" for everything because they don't want to tell the boss "no". Yet they'll bend over backwards doing things that perhaps should have no place in any sane or normal business environment. But since they won't say anything, you need to find another objective set of eyes, and another set of shoulders to lean on. Employees who say "yes" to everything can be costly. Also, being an entrepreneur can be incredibly lonely, as you'll be the one making all the decisions, and people will be counting on you for everything. Fortunately, I got smart and hired a couple of great business coaches who focus on different aspects of my businesses.

   LESSON LEARNED: Get an advisor, and skip some pitfalls. Sure I have an MBA. And I have experience. A lot of experience. But an objective set of eyes is an amazing thing. I should have listened to my advisor on a few things much sooner than I did.

3. **BEING TOO NICE.** I'm not saying to be a real bitch. But sometimes people have taken advantage of the fact that I am nice. Whether it's taking time off from work, or not quite being as accountable as they should be, I've seen a few instances of this.

   LESSON LEARNED: Draw the line, and call people on it when they cross it. Set expectations, and don't allow people to take advantage of you. Track time that employees are working, when they come into the office, and when they leave. You may find that they are taking a little bit here, and a little bit there, and next thing you know, they aren't getting any real work done.

I'm sure that I've made plenty of other mistakes in my businesses, and it is just a question of figuring out what they are, and how to correct them. I know that no matter how well things seem to be going at any given point in time, there are always things I could be doing better than I am right now.

Knowing When to Say "No" as an Entrepreneur

Business owners have many opportunities arise. The challenge is choosing the right ones. Good opportunities will enhance your company. If it doesn't enhance what you're doing, or get you closer to your goals, you should say no.

Too many entrepreneurs never learn to say, 'NO!'. In an effort to get their business off the ground and keep it up and running, they say 'yes' to everything. They end up trying to do too much for too many, which dilutes their focus and often the quality of their product or service. Don't let this happen to you.

The desire to say yes to everything is understandable, but that doesn't make it right or productive. If you're an entrepreneur (or an aspiring entrepreneur), here is why saying "no" can actually be one of the most important words in your vocabulary.

The Dangers of Saying "Yes"

Nearly everyone has experienced the harmful side effects of saying yes too often: wasting time, burning out, and being over-committed with your time. When you're exhausted, your business is not going to run at its best. Saying yes too often can cause you to become unfocused on the important tasks in your business. At worst, it can become a bad habit that leads to bad decisions that can cause massive disorder in your business. It will cause you to react to the latest offer you said yes to rather than chasing the original goals you intended when you started your business.

Once you have started saying yes to everything that crosses your path, you've relinquished control over your business direction. If you allow the priorities of others to come first, you're short-changing your own priorities, and your business is likely to go astray. Then you will sacrifice the very benefits you were chasing as an entrepreneur in the first place. Your time and priorities will come second to others' when you are always saying yes to everything that is handed your way.

There are too many unhappy entrepreneurs who built their businesses by suggestions and requests of others instead of using their own business ideas. Instead of saying no to others' ideas or requests, they said yes and ended up running businesses they didn't necessarily like. It's important to learn now that saying yes to everything might start as a small problem, but can end up as a big one.

Learning How to Say "No"

Learning how to say a simple 2-letter word isn't as easy as it may seem, so you have to change the way you think about it. You have to change your entire mindset about the word "no." No is not a negative. In fact, it's a way to protect three of the things that you love most: your business, your life and your sanity.

You must remind yourself that every favor, phone call, extra client, coffee, meeting, or other unnecessary business, takes away from the things you want and really need to be doing. That time can really add up. Every difficult or underpaying client takes away time that you can be spending on better, nicer and higher paying, more rewarding clients, which can add value to your business. Each unnecessary opportunity takes away valuable resources and time from the projects that really can advance your business.

It's important to remind yourself that by saying no, you are actually saying YES to the things that truly deserve your attention and time, so you'll have time for the best opportunities for your business when they come. That by saying no, you're able to keep the clients you have and love, and give them the attention they deserve. Only by saying no are you truly able to be the entrepreneur you dreamed of being and doing rewarding work on your own time and your own terms.

Have you learned to say "no" or are you still working on this part of your business? How can you use this 2-letter word more efficiently?

Everyone Needs a Mentor

Women are not very good at finding mentors, especially other women who are mentors. Mostly, they think that they don't have time, or that other mentors aren't like them, so they don't understand their concerns and problems.

If you're a woman who is an entrepreneur, you're in a very small minority. Finding someone who can understand where you're coming from may seem really daunting, and maybe it just isn't worth it, since it's likely to be a lot of work. I mean, why bother, if it's not easy?

It is especially easy to fall into this trap if you're doing well, and everyone around you is telling you how well you are doing. I will step out here and say that everyone needs a mentor or coach. I'm actually working with a couple of different coaches and mentors on different businesses and aspects of my business.

10 Things a Coach Can Do For You:

1. **THEY CAN SEE THINGS THAT YOU CAN'T.** They're on the outside looking in, and can point out the obvious that sometimes can be easy to miss when you're standing there in the middle of it all.

2. **THEY WILL TELL YOU NO.** Most employees are motivated to please, and thus will not want to tell you when they think you're making a bad move. A good coach or mentor will tell you when you're messing up.

3. **RESOURCES.** If you need introductions or resources, a coach can help you find resources to grow your business more quickly.

4. **THEY CAN HELP YOU AVOID MISTAKES.** If you choose a coach with business experience, they can help you side-step costly mistakes. Every

business coach has a different focus, so you can work with different people at different points in time to address specific issues.

5. **HELP YOU SAVE MONEY.** Spending money to save money may sound idiotic or like an oxymoron. My business coaches have had ideas that have saved me far more than the cost of their coaching.

6. **GROW YOUR BUSINESS FASTER.** Wouldn't you like to become profitable faster, and grow your business faster?

7. Hold you accountable. To me, it's good to know I've got someone watching and holding me accountable for my actions.

8. **HELP YOU GET YOUR BUSINESS HOUSE IN ORDER.** From making sure that all of the business basics are covered, to accounting, proper payroll setup, and more, they can help you make sure you're not missing something critical.

9. **BE A GREAT SET OF EARS WHEN YOU JUST NEED SOMEONE TO LISTEN AND NOT JUDGE.** Let's face it, most of us don't have many friends who have been in business. And you may not want them to know about mistakes you've made, or problems you're having. A good coach will listen to your problems, and they won't judge. Chances are, they've been there themselves.

10. **HELP YOU PRIORITIZE TASKS.** Sometimes there's just so much to do, that you don't know where to start. A good coach will understand your goals, and can help you figure out what you need to do first, and what you can just not do at all.

A coach can't fix every problem you're ever going to have, but they can sure save you a lot of scrapes and bumps along the road. I think every businessperson should have a mentor or coach, and that goes doubly so for every entrepreneur.

Find the right person who is compatible with your goals and desires.

THE BASICS OF BUSINESS OPERATIONS

Do You Need an MBA to Start a Business?

I think one of the biggest misconceptions is that to start a business you need a fancy education. Sure, I do have an MBA from a top-rated business school, and it has helped me tremendously; I acquired a lot of skills. Some of those skills can be applied directly to small businesses and entrepreneurship, and quite a few can't. The MBA is great for high-level stuff, like accounting, finance, strategy, and operations management, but it doesn't focus on the nitty-gritty details of starting a business. If your desire is to simply start a business, then a few business and accounting classes may be what you really need, rather than the entire program.

What you really need are these things:

1. RESOURCES, including online resources and coursework specifically targeted at starting a business, and a business coach that will help you stay focused. A good business coach will also give you objective advice that may not always be what you want to hear, but will be what you NEED to hear. I've found that this is critical, because employees and friends might tell you things to be nice. That can be a bad thing, because it can lead you to make decisions that aren't in your best interest. A good coach will tell you, 'No', on occasion, give you a pep talk when you need it, and stick with you through it, giving you a bit of their experience and strength.

2. **PERSISTENCE.** You have to start the business, and stick with it to see it become successful. The likelihood that a business will succeed improves dramatically when you stick with it. That may mean sticking with it for years before you see the kind of return you'd like to see, and learning from your lumps. But by doing #1, and getting objective feedback that you implement, you can learn the lessons faster, and become profitable that much sooner.   Some days, business is not going to be easy. In our business, it may be that a lucrative client goes into the hospital, or even dies, and no longer needs service. Sometimes we have clients who are very, very challenging, and we may not be able to meet their needs. Those situations are temporary setbacks, because there are always more clients out there who desperately need our services. We just need to find them. It's about being persistent, and not quitting when something goes wrong.

If you are persistent, and really stick with it, and get good information from great resources, you will very likely succeed. The odds will be in your favor because you'll be getting the kind of support you need. Coupled with persistence, these are an unbeatable combination.

Why Care About Business Basics?

Many times when entrepreneurs start a business, they just hop in with both feet, and figure out what they're going to sell, and get going. They really don't spend the time to figure out their business basics. What are those business basics I'm speaking of?

Business basics are things like setting up separate bank accounts, a filing system, accounting systems, incorporation, insurance, and all the nitty-gritty parts of running a business. They are the operations portions of a business and business setup, and they are critical for a business' success, yet many entrepreneurs don't want to be bothered to take the time to focus on taking care of these details.

I can tell lots of hair-raising stories, as can others in business, of business owners who failed to set up their accounting systems, and who ended up spending thousands of dollars in extra accounting fees to finally get their accounting set up. I've heard of home care owners who ended up owing hundreds of thousands of dollars for failing to set up their employees as W-2 employees. Let's stop there for a minute. Hundreds of thousands of dollars owed to the government just for not paying attention and setting things up right the first time. That would definitely not make me happy, and could cost me my business.

I can go on for a long time with stories of people who ended up with fines, who nearly lost their businesses, or actually did lose their businesses, for silly things like not bothering to set up an accounting system, separate bank accounts, or a corporate entity. Quite simply, they failed to set up their business basics appropriately. Don't let this be you. If you think that saving a few hundred bucks because you are so desperate for the money is a good idea, then I beg you to please reconsider. Your business and livelihood could depend on it.

Business Basics Everyone Needs:

- **INCORPORATION.** If you are operating a business serving other people, or selling things, you should consult an attorney about incorporating your business to separate your own finances from the business. This also provides a level of legal protection for your own personal finances. Most people set up an LLC for this purpose, and it separates your company from your own finances.

- **TAX ID.** If you incorporate, the business will have its own tax ID. You'll use that for opening a business bank account.

- **SEPARATE BANK ACCOUNTS.** Keep your business bank accounts separate from your personal accounts. You need to do this so that you don't end up giving the IRS a free loan, and so that you can grow your business. This is also valuable if you ever decide to sell.

  The other benefit to having completely separate bank accounts (and not dipping into company bank accounts constantly) is that you provide a better degree of legal protection to your assets in case of a lawsuit. No one wants to ever think about this happening to them, but it can and does happen. Protect yourself, and consult an attorney, so you can get this stuff set up.

- **ACCOUNTING SYSTEM.** If you don't have an accounting system, even if it's just a spreadsheet, you have given the government a free loan, as you won't be able to track your own expenses and income. Setting up Quickbooks is super quick, and is also very inexpensive. If doing the books isn't your thing, you can hire someone to do them for you. Mostly, you should be able to import information from your bank accounts, and payroll system (if you have one) and categorize it.

- **FILING SYSTEM.** You need to be able to figure out where you stored things, so a good filing system that makes sense to you is super important. In our first couple of years in business, we didn't have an official office, so we were storing files in people's homes. I cannot tell you how many financial files were misplaced and had to be re-created. This cost us a lot of money.

- **MILEAGE TRACKER.** Keep a log of all of your mileage for your business. Seriously, if I could go back and do this one over, I would.

I have logged thousands of miles in my car that I didn't manage to track correctly. That has meant thousands of dollars that I've given up for free because I didn't manage to track them. In two years, that has added up to at least $5000, given the amount that I'm driving. I know I could certainly use that money in my pocket, and it seems silly to just give it away, yet I've done that. There are some simple apps you can install on your phone to track mileage, and it takes less than 10 minutes a month to categorize all your driving.

- **OFFICE SPACE.** Whether this space is in your home, or in a separate office, you need to have office space. It should have dedicated filing areas. And you need to be able to keep track of all the things that are associated with your business, and keep them separate from everything else. You need to have copies of all of your legal documents, tax ID, unemployment tax paperwork, etc. The other benefit of a dedicated office space is that you will go into work mode when you enter that space. For me, it is important to separate work from play in my mind. By having an office space outside the home, we can have clients come into the office to meet with us, so there is benefit to having an office outside the home.

By setting up your business foundations and basics, you are setting your business up to succeed. I firmly believe that business is about persistence, and making sure that you're doing all the right things to be a legitimate business.

Tips for Great Business Process

One thing I've seen in various companies I've worked for is that each and every company has its own culture and its on set of processes. Not every process is a great business process, so how do you make it easily remembered, repeatable, consistent, and easy to follow? Remember that the easier the process is to follow, the more likely that an employee is going to follow that process.

How is the result of a great business process achieved?

5 Tips for Great Business Process

1. **CREATE A SET OF CHEAT SHEETS** or cheat cards that employees can study or refer back to, something like flash cards. Create a binder just for your process sheets so that anyone can pick up a job by reading the notes on the cards.

2. **MAKE IT HARD FOR PEOPLE TO NOT FOLLOW THE PROCESS.** This is all about decision management. If a process requires daily caring and feeding, make sure that employees know that, and that they understand the importance of that caring and feeding to their eco-system.

   One example I can give is client notes. We have made it clear that caregivers must complete their client notes, and turn them in weekly. For incentive, if the caregiver doesn't turn in notes, then they will have to come to the office to pick up a paper check, rather than having their check electronically deposited into their account. Most people manage to turn in their paperwork after the first time this happens.

3. **BE CONSISTENT, AND MODEL THE PROCESS YOURSELF.** If you want something done a particular way, the best way to accomplish that it is to make it so others can emulate you and your process. You should

walk the walk, and be consistent. That means, being into work early in the morning, and staying late where applicable. If your employees see you breezing into the office at 10 AM, and leaving at 3 PM, you can bet that they will do the same. If you are sloppy in your file handling, they will be too.

4. **CREATE FLOW CHARTS TO GIVE A META VIEW OF THE PROCESS.** Flow charts help people visualize the process. People tend to do better when they have a visual representation of what they are doing so that they can follow along.

5. **USE SCRIPTS FOR PARTS OF THE PROCESS THAT WORK WELL WITH SCRIPTS.** If I know that I want my employees to always answer the phone a particular way, I will print out what I want them to say, laminate it, and stick it in front of them to read every time they answer the phone. I'll also make sure that we have a proper data entry form (either paper or computer) for them to take down notes about the call and handle it correctly, including call back information and referral source. We had to make sure that the questionnaire we used when the phone is answered correctly mirrors the forms in the database.

Business process is critical to having a functioning business. This is especially true as you add clients. The truth of the matter is that our human minds want to do well by our clients, but when it comes down to it, we don't always manage to follow the same steps every time, which is what it takes for consistently great outcomes. Whether it's a client intake form, your process for billing clients, or just the way you answer the phone, document it, and make it consistent.

Plan, Test, Plan, Test, and So On

One of the fun things I'm doing with my home care business is planning, and then testing out how things work, then planning some more. It is a never-ending cycle, which will never result in perfection, but hopefully will result in a viable, healthy home care business.

The key to this testing cycle is that it is very short. We don't take forever to start a new process, but rather we do things quickly to see if it will work. If the test doesn't work, then we get rid of it and move onto something different. Examples of this include using particular companies for SEO (search engine optimization), or for PPC (pay-per-click) on Google. We tried them for short periods (a month or two or three), and if they don't work, they're gone.

We quickly discovered that very few things go quite to plan. For instance, we tried to set up payroll, but couldn't use starter checks for that. So we had to find another way to do it. Worker's comp is brutally expensive, so we had to find a way to pay a graduated fee so that we don't burn through all of our cash in one sitting. Little things like that which make the business go around. We have learned a lot of lessons about workman's comp, like the fact that many companies require you to be in business for 3 years before they will give you a quote.

Plan. Test. Analyze. See what works and what doesn't. Plan, test. Plan, test. It's an endless loop that goes around and around.

Learn quickly from your mistakes and move on. Don't allow yourself to get mired down trying to plan out things to the nth degree if they don't require that degree of planning. Try things quickly, and move on. If you're a small business, there is no reason that small actions should take long periods of time. Very few things in small business should take months to implement.

I think that no business ever quite works as advertised, or as planned in the timelines originally planned for. That is okay. It's about adapting to ever-changing conditions, and educating ourselves to handle the conditions to the best of our ability.

In the end we will be successful; we just need to keep plugging away at the problems.

Answer the #$%& Phone!

If I can give any entrepreneur one piece of advice, it is this: Answer the phone. You need to have a consistent way to answer all of the calls you get, and follow up on those calls. Ditto for emails that you may receive. Every time you get an email or phone call from a prospective client, treat it like gold.

Okay, so you have lots of calls coming in and they are preventing you from getting your work done, and you don't know how to handle them. That's a fantastic problem to have. You have to manage those calls, though. How you decide to manage the call volume can depend on what your goals are, and how you want the individual calls to be handled.

3 Ways to Handle Calls

1. The easiest way to handle calls is to answer the phone yourself. Carry your cell phone and a calendar book everywhere. Make appointments and follow up yourself. Of course, if you're already overwhelmed, this could tip you over the edge.

2. Get a live answering service. We've used Ruby Receptionist, and have been extremely pleased. This ensures that the calls are answered in just a few seconds. And we quit having issues with dropped calls, or it taking a while to connect the call, and the client thinking we weren't going to answer the call. Answering Services act just like a receptionist, and you can tell them exactly how to handle each type of call. Best points - they know when a call is spam, and can treat it appropriately, because as a business owner, other people will try to call you and sell you lots of things. One caveat for this is that if you don't get a great answering service, your customers won't be happy with you.

3. Get an assistant or virtual assistant. One of the hottest things going is to hire a virtual assistant or a part time assistant to help with scheduling, returning calls, answering phones, and more. There are lots of people out there looking for positions, and this can be very helpful. You have an almost unlimited variety of people to choose from, as well as different modalities. I've hired moms, seniors, and people who are just looking for part time work. ODesk offers Virtual Assistants, and there are other offshore assistants that can perform a huge variety of tasks to keep you on track. You just have to decide exactly how you want your phone answered, and make it happen.

None of these options have to be very expensive. Note that you can get support from an answering service for a couple hundred dollars per month. A virtual assistant in the Philippines working 40 or so hours a week is also just a couple hundred dollars per month. So, research your choices, and choose something. Don't over spend, but make sure that you answer the phone. Clients can't reach you, and your business can't grow if you don't answer the phone!

Entrepreneur Tip: Get an Office

One of the lessons I learned the hard way is that if you have an employee, or there are two or more of you, having office space is invaluable. There are business incubators that offer a variety of office packages, including a single office with a phone, and that will give you a mailing address.

Reasons You Need to Get an Office:

- **ACCOUNTABILITY** – You will have a much better idea of how long people are working and what they're up to. If you don't see people in the office, then they could be out on calls with clients, or they could just be not working at all, but do you know which it is? Having an office makes it much easier to tell. Got an employee routinely coming in late, and leaving super early? How will you know if they're working from home? How do you know if the time that they are working is the least bit productive?

- **TEAM BUILDING** – Have you ever had a team that was located all over the place, and with no one in the same building? Was it terribly hard to work together? I believe that humans need to be face to face to work together optimally. Otherwise, you will have mistrust and miscommunication. To get people to come together, you have to get them together. If you have any employees, you need to spend time together, communicating. That is part of the overhead of having more than one employee.

- **REMOVE REDUNDANCY** – When we moved into our office, we found that we had a 5-year supply of all of our printed supplies, multiple printers, and more. By consolidating into a single location, you can remove redundancies in the workplace, and in your life.

Not convinced? Are you still thinking that it's best to work remotely? That's fine. But have you asked your employees what they think? Or what environment they want to work in? In some cases, if they are a go-getter, then they will tell you that they need to work in an office.

Still not convinced? Well, let me tell you the story about the brochures. When we moved to our new office in January, everyone started bringing in the brochures that they had in their cars, home offices, and strewn across the county. The boxes started coming, and kept coming. We had thousands and thousands of brochures that were already in people's hands that hadn't been handed out. That represents several thousand dollars worth of brochures that we had bought, because we thought we needed more. Of course, if you don't have employees, this might not be an issue for you, but if you have several people on your staff, and are a quickly growing business, it could be a very real issue.

You would be surprised at all the things we discovered after we moved and started going over our finances, records and resources.

GETTING & KEEPING CLIENTS

Know Who Your Ideal Client Is

In almost every business, there is an image of who the ideal client is. In my home care agency, it may be someone who needs a moderate amount of care – say 15-20 hours per week, is about 80 years old, and likely female. For my business coaching, my ideal client is different – usually a woman, aged between 30 and 45, who wants some help with a business that she's starting, or has just started, and needs help getting it off the ground. She is likely well educated, and has a ton of fantastic experience, but not necessarily experience with entrepreneurship in particular. Every business has their ideal clients. You should know exactly who your ideal client is.

What does your ideal client like? What are their hobbies? Where do they hang out? What is their income, education, and what are their demographics? Is your ideal client male or female? Are you going to be dealing directly with the client? Or will you have to deal indirectly, by working with the client's children? Knowing that information about your client will give you clear clues on where to go to find them.

One really good example that I can give you is that in my home care business, many of my ideal clients live on Facebook. They don't live on Snapchat. So, of course, I'm not going to spend my time on Snapchat. I also know that I'm likely to find them online, so I make sure that I have a strong online presence for my business. In fact, I believe that if my ideal client is given a referral for my services, they will in many cases go and Google my company and look for reviews online. In order to have credibility with that audience, it's necessary to have a significant presence online, or we might as well be invisible.

Try to get inside the head of your ideal client, and understand who that person is, and what they want. It's even better if you understand WHY they want something. Know why they want to be able to find you online. In my case, it's because most women are super, super busy, and just don't have time to go around looking for things. And if they pick up the phone, they are likely interested in doing business; Generation X doesn't pick up the phone unless they're serious. I know that the phone must be answered, because they're going to go somewhere else if I don't answer that phone. I work with a great answering service, so we don't miss any calls!

So many pieces of information are available to us, and if we think through who our ideal client is, and why they do things, it becomes easier to sell to that client. Once you know who that person is, and what they want, you can use their language to sell to them. Win!

Tips for Getting More Clients

I think that just about every business needs more clients. I know mine does, and I'm sure that yours does too, if you're a business owner. Think about where your clients are coming from, and work the most profitable ones. I'm going to make the possibly erroneous assumption here that you're already providing a great product or service.

Getting More Clients

1. You need to work your network. Ask family, friends, contacts on LinkedIn, and all of your social media. Don't just broadcast the request. You need to talk to each person one on one, or email them a custom email, asking them for help for referrals.

2. Go to your current clients, and ask them if they know of anyone who might use your service or products.

3. Write a thank you note to your past and current clients; thank them for doing business with you. Be sure to ask them for a referral. You should make sure your contact information is somewhere either on the envelope or on the back of the card, but don't put a business card into the envelope. It is especially advantageous to do this very shortly after you've provided a service.

4. Use social media to your advantage. Figure out what social media you want to use, and focus on that. Most potential clients are going to Google you. They want to see what the online reviews say.

5. Focus on building an email list. You can use your current customers' email addresses to start the list. Then send regular communication. Think that this doesn't apply to you? Well, how much more likely are you to go get your oil changed if you get reminded to do it every so often? How about spring-cleaning? How about if we talk about

spring-cleaning, and give you tips to do it, then ask you if you'd like to schedule to have us come in and perform those services? I think that almost any business can benefit from this. If you're not great at doing it yourself, hire a Virtual Assistant who can do it for you on a consistent and regular basis. You want to deliver quality content in a predictable manner that will make people want to open your next email.

6. Put together a mobile friendly website with all the pertinent information on it, including how to contact you. If you are in an industry where photos are appropriate, then post pictures. I think that pictures or videos are priceless.

7. After you've sold your product or service, check to make sure the client is satisfied, and if not, do what it takes to get them there.

8. Focus on delivering a consistent experience every time. Your clients want to know what to expect, and know that they're going to get consistently good results. If you put processes and procedures in place to ensure that they always get the experience they are expecting, they will be much more likely to refer others to you.

9. Don't leave without at least trying to set up the next appointment or next sale. If you clean houses, then set up the next appointment before you leave. If you clean chimneys, then go ahead and set up the next service appointment, or set up a reminder system, so that people don't use your product or service once, and then forget about you. You want to stay front of minds.

10. Figure out where your ideal client lives, what they do, and how they live. Then put yourself in their path. In home care, we get most of our referrals from certain types of sources, so we approach those sources regularly. I've also found certain groups on the Internet where my target audience resides, so I spend a lot of time there.

If you can follow these steps, you'll add clients quickly. I will add one bonus though, which is probably the most important one of all:

Answer your phone and emails, return calls and reply to emails super quickly! You can get all the clients in the world calling you, but if you don't answer your phone, they are worthless. We learned that in sales, answering the phone is priceless; if you can't do that, return the call as quickly as possible. In this case, time is money. That isn't a cliché, and studies have shown that if you don't return a call or call an internet lead in the first 10 minutes, then your chances of getting them as a client drop exponentially. The more time that has passed since the initial call, the less likely you are to get the client. The numbers are truly stunning. Following through with the sale is critical to getting it!

It's all About Sales

One of the biggest realizations I have come to in business is that it's all about sales. Everything we do hinges on sales. If you don't get out and tell the world about your product or service, and make a sustained effort to tell the world about it, then you will die in obscurity. Sales is one of the key foundations of business; you need buyers to buy your product or service. People need to know who you are, what you do, and what you can do for them, before they will ever begin to consider doing business with you. They have to know you first, then like you, then begin to trust you.

Telling family and friends about your company is a good first step, but it's not the only one that you need to take. The people closest to you will be your biggest advocates, but you need to reach out beyond your inner circles to truly be successful.

I had the realization about 4 months into owning my home care agency that I was going to need to seriously step up sales for the entire company if we were going to grow the way I wanted us to. That meant me, and every single staff member. We had to learn that everyone is responsible for sales, and for the client's experience, from the first time they reach us on the phone until we sign them, and through the entire process.

Since Extension of You is a Home Care agency, we have opportunities along the way to upsell, or increase our service. It's up to us to deliver that exemplary service, and ask for more. If everyone on my staff is working together on this, then it's not a big deal. But as soon as anyone loses sight of the fact that our clients need constant love and attention, we lose business.

This is also true for Leadership Girl. I've had the blog, and been doing some business coaching for a while now. I realized that I needed to seriously step up my game to publicize the blog, the posts, and the information we're sharing. In short, I needed to be making a much more concerted effort to introduce myself to more people as a business coach, since it's about helping more people than just the people in my circle of acquaintances. In order to help those people, they have to get to know, like, and trust me to be willing to do business with me.

After all, you're not going to hire a business coach you don't know anything about, and you're certainly not going to just stumble out there and find me on the internet, if I don't make a point of building back links and improving my SEO. I have to put myself out there, and SELL my products and services, in a knowledgeable way, that isn't overwhelming or pushy. It's a lot of work, and it's a lot of sales.

I came to the realization somewhere along the way that business lives or dies by sales, and that it's all about sales, and making those sales over and over again, until the business is a success.

Easy Things You Can Do To Grow your Business

There are lots of people out there right now looking to buy whatever it is that your business is selling, but they don't know about you, or your product or service. That is absolutely true whether you are cleaning houses, or whether you are a travel agent, real estate agent, or a business coach, life coach, or any other business. So, how do you close that gap right now to get in front of those people?

What are some easy, inexpensive things that you can do right now to tell the world about your business?

1. **CREATE A FACEBOOK BUSINESS PAGE,** and put pictures up. Then invite your friends and family to like and share it. Your family and friends are your team, and they naturally are going to want to help you out. You need to ask those family and friends for help to build your business. The better the content, and the more engaging it is, the easier it will be to get people to like your Facebook page. Notice that I didn't say that you should boost your content, although that will get it seen by more people. You really need to simply focus on creating quality content, and asking people to share it. If you ask regularly (but not obnoxiously), then people will be much more likely to share your content.

2. **ADD YOUR BUSINESS TO YOUR FACEBOOK PROFILE.** Easy, right? Yet, how many of us just think that Facebook is for friends, and don't link to our business that way? You're doing yourself, and your potential customers, a disservice. I'm not saying that you should promote your business in every other post, but you certainly should make your business known to people who know you. Otherwise, how can they

begin to support you? Usually your first customers are going to come from the family and friends circle, and that is a good thing.

3. **ADD YOUR BUSINESS TO YOUR EMAIL SIGNATURE.** This one is also super easy. Put a link on all of your email signatures, so that people can see what you do. It doesn't have to be fancy, but tell the world what you do – they DO notice. I can't tell you how many comments I get about my signature, and about quotes in my signature. I will change the quotes in my signature every once in a while to see if people are paying attention, and funnily enough, people do notice and comment on the quotes that I put in my signatures quite often. I also get people following me on LinkedIn, Pinterest and Twitter just by including that information in my email signatures.

4. **BUILD RELATIONSHIPS IN YOUR COMMUNITY.** People buy from those they know, like and trust. They have to have a relationship with you, or perceive that they do, in order for them to want to do this. That may mean figuring out where your target demographic hangs out, and putting yourself there by volunteering, hanging out, and otherwise being a presence. For some people, church, or their place of worship may be a good choice. For other people, networking groups will be a great place. For my senior home care business, networking groups are for the most part, a waste of time. But for my business coaching, networking groups are where my ideal clients live.

5. **FACEBOOK GROUPS.** Find Facebook groups where your target demographic hangs out, and hang out there too. Never, ever do drive-by postings about your business, but instead become a trusted resource. If you don't have time to make a meaningful contribution, do NOT use this method. You need to make sure that you contribute lots of helpful information, and become a community resource in order to use this method effectively.

6. **MAGNETS ON YOUR CAR, ESPECIALLY THE BACK AND SIDES.** I get stopped regularly in the drive-through by people asking me if I am with the business on the magnets on the side of my car. I've gotten clients that way. How easy is that? Make sure that the information is visible from a good distance, and that the magnets are colorful. Another tip I have is that you should make sure to wash your car, and then replace the magnets every week or two. Otherwise, it can become

fused to your vehicle's paint, which can cause quite an ugly mess. So, make sure you lift those magnets, and clean under them, to keep your car looking good. One other caveat. If you're going to plaster your company's information to the outside of your car, please drive like you know that your information is posted. Otherwise, you may be creating enemies, and turning them against your business. Since that's not helpful, just keep an eye out.

7. **CARRY BUSINESS CARDS.** You can order business cards super cheap from Vistaprint, and should carry them with you wherever you go. Hand them out like candy. A nice business card, done well, will get you plenty of clients. Make sure that it looks good, and that you share your cards. One note about business cards. You should never take someone's information from their card, and add them to your email list for your business. This is a violation of most terms and conditions, and can cause you to face significant fines. It turns people off of your business, and can be a very costly mistake.

8. **WRITE THANK YOU NOTES TO CURRENT CLIENTS, AND ASK FOR REFERRALS.** After you perform a service or sell something to someone, ask them to refer someone else to you if they liked your service. If you don't ask, you won't receive! People are thrilled to receive an old-fashioned thank you note in the mail. One thing that is worth mentioning here. People tend to prefer custom thank you notes, and not something with your logo plastered on it. I have a friend who makes beautiful hand made cards, and I use those in many instances. For the rest, I use simple, regular thank you notes from Target, or another local store. Pretty cards are better, but it's not necessary to spend a fortune here.

9. **USE LINKEDIN TO NETWORK.** It's amazing how many people you've probably worked with in the past, and how many people you know in the community. Use LinkedIn to connect to people and reach out to them for business. On LinkedIn, you can join various communities, and post articles and information that are pertinent to your industry. This will help you become established as a thought leader in your industry. LinkedIn also allows you to publish articles. You can use this opportunity to point back to your website, and even reuse content that you've previously published on your blog.

10. **Ask Your Friends and Families for Referrals.** Your friends and family will be your biggest advocates, and they will be your first customers. Make sure you are asking them for those referrals!

11. **Use Pinterest to Market your Products and Services.** Seriously, Pinterest is an amazing tool that you can use to bundle up different pieces of information about your businesses. If you make the pictures amazing, people will share and re-pin your information all over the place. How cool is that? And, it can be perfectly free, which is my dream price, for sure.

12. **Create Videos Using Your Laptop Camera.** There are lots of inexpensive ways to create videos, from using your laptop camera, to just running a Google hangout and recording it. If you have video content, it becomes much easier to market your business, especially if you have short videos.

13. **Instagram.** Instagram is a powerhouse for marketing things graphically. You may think that you have a business that doesn't lend itself well to graphics, but with a bit of creativity, you can market nearly anything graphically. We've done that with Home Care and Business Coaching, so I'm pretty sure nearly anything can be done.

14. **Hoof it.** Figure out who your ideal referral services are, and pay them a visit. You'll be amazed at how likely people are to refer to you, if you just get out and ask for the business. This won't work well for all businesses, but it does work quite well for a number of different ones.

15. **100 Call Challenge.** This one works well on a snow day, or when you can't otherwise get out of the house. Start at 8:30 AM, and start calling people, asking who they might know who needs your service. I bet that you will find clients doing this. I've seen it work for Realtors, house-keepers, accountants, and home care.

Simple Techniques You Can Use to Make Money Now

Most businesses need more money. There are probably 1000 things you want to do now for your business, all of which would probably benefit it. In this article, we're going to talk about 7 simple techniques you can use now to make money so that you can start doing those things for your business - because you need to make money to support yourself, and your family, without spending a lot of money.

Techniques You Can Use Now to Make Money

1. SELL INTRODUCTORY PACKAGES, at a price that's a no-brainer for most of your prospective clients, and let people know that they're available.

2. FIND FACEBOOK GROUPS that have your ideal clients in them, and become a member, and where permissible, list your offerings for sale.

3. RUN A SALE. Most people love a really good sale, so do a great sale, and make sure that you let the world know about it.

4. ASK FRIENDS AND FAMILY members who they know who might want or need your service or product. This is most effective if you speak to them one at a time, rather than spray and pray.

5. THE 100 CALL CHALLENGE. This one is a doozy, but it works. Challenge yourself to call 100 people in a day, and ask who they know who might need your product or service. Start early in the morning, and work through the day. Make sure you share it on Facebook and other social media outlets so people can help you reach your goal.

6. ATTEND COMMUNITY NETWORKING MEETINGS, leads groups, BNI groups, and more. The more you put yourself out there, the faster your business will grow.

7. **JOIN YOUR LOCAL CHAMBER OF COMMERCE,** if the price is reasonable. Then approach the other chamber members with your product or service. Most people want to support a local small business.

Know that growing your business is doable, but it will likely take more work than you expect it to. People will do business with those who they know, like and trust, so the quicker you can build those relationships (without seeming creepy), the faster your business will grow.

Increase the Money in Your Pocket!

One of the simplest rules of business is that if you want to increase the money in your pocket, you have to follow a simple rule - increase sales or decrease expenses. It's that easy. Or is it? Is it like dieting, where you need to eat less, and exercise more? Where it sounds deadly simple, but the reality is actually not so simple?

Let me see if I can explain. In business, there are expenses associated with increasing sales, otherwise known as the cost of goods sold, and overhead. There is a relatively fixed amount of overhead for many companies - things like rent and office staff. The things that don't change much because they are fixed costs are generally called overhead.

Cost of goods sold is a bit more tricky to calculate, because you have to factor a little bit of the overhead into each unit sold. You also need to factor in things like the amount of time that an item spends in the warehouse, the cost of the item, marketing, materials, manufacturing, and the myriad of details that go into it. One thing I learned in Business School is that this is an art form, and not an exact science, so there are many ways to figure out the cost of goods sold, depending on what your goals are.

Where things start to get a bit dicey is when you start having to add overhead, or increase your client acquisition cost in order to get the next client. So, if you need to add extra office staff, increase your office size, or increase advertising, you increase your overhead, so the marginal cost of that next item sold increases dramatically. It's those inflection points that can be killers. If you don't watch for them when growing your business, suddenly you can have a lot less money in your pocket. You can actually be losing money instead because you can exceed income in so many tricky ways.

Of course, the easiest way is to just keep growing and manage costs carefully along the way, watching what the marginal costs are doing to your bottom line. So, go ahead and increase your sales, and decrease expenses where it makes common sense to do so. Your business will be healthier for it. But please don't do any crazy cost-cutting measures that will drive everyone crazy!

Growing Your Business Face to Face

One of the most effective ways to grow your business is by doing cold calls, or meeting people face to face. This method can work extremely well when done correctly, and it can work extremely poorly if you don't do the right things. It's important to understand that when you are calling on people, the goal is to build a relationship with the right people, and to help solve their problems. Most of them aren't going to magically give you leads, or give you money out of the goodness of their hearts. You have to establish that "know, like and trust" factor.

11 Tips to Grow Your Business Face To Face

1. Networking meetings may be a good way to start, but they are not where you want to spend most of your time. People come to those meetings to meet people, and get leads. Most of them never get a single lead. Those meetings are great for a card grab, and you can then set up a follow-up meeting.

2. People aren't going to just give you their business, or leads. You might get lucky that someone out there will give you a shot, but most of the time, you are going to have to build your relationship with the "know, like, trust" factor. That means taking time. That means it can take 6 months or longer to break into an account.

3. Being pushy isn't going to get you anywhere. People don't like being sold to, and they especially don't like being pushed around. You have to be genuine, and real.

4. No name dropping, unless someone specifically introduced you. Just because you know my cousin, or best friend, doesn't mean I'm predisposed to like you or your business. Furthermore, if you come

on too strong, and name drop, people are going to drop you like a hot poker.

5. Tandem marketing or sales can be a good strategy. Sometimes if you're trying to get into an account, and get past the gatekeeper, it may be easier if two of you go. It's not as easy to be rude to someone if there are two of you present.

6. Where possible, network, and get your friends to introduce you. This works so much better than name dropping, and is much more likely to give rise to a warm lead.

7. You have to get out and make a LOT of face to face calls. By a lot of calls, that means 60-90 calls per week, depending on the business. Additionally, you will need to make phone calls. Get yourself geared up for seeing lots and lots of people, over and over again.

8. You have to be consistent. For your top accounts, you need to go back as much as a few times per week. For other accounts, you may only go back a couple times per year. You need to have the accounts on a set schedule, where you decide how often to go back and visit them. Often times people won't give you a referral the first 10 or so times you meet with them. Most sales people are going to give up after the first couple of meetings without results. The most successful sales people will be those who keep going after what they want, politely and kindly. That may mean dozens of meetings with people before they know, like, and trust you enough to give you any business.

9. Constant research is a must. Businesses come and go, and the people at those businesses come and go, which means that there is constant churn, and there are constant opportunities. We like to joke in the senior long term care industry that sales reps change jobs like they change socks. That means that they may be gone from one location today, and pop up tomorrow in another location. Thus, you need to know who is going where, and to know multiple people at each company you visit.

10. Ask everyone you meet who else they know who might need your services. I think that you'll be delightfully surprised at how well they respond, and how many referrals you get just by asking.

11. Once you have established a rapport, you need to ask for the business. Going by and visiting is lovely and all, but you need to ask for that business, or you're never going to get it. With Girl Scout Cookies, we stand in front of stores freezing our butts off. There have been countless times where we've asked for the sale, and people have turned around and bought from us, who were otherwise not aware, or who had decided to ignore us. That has added up to thousands of boxes of cookies sold over the years. The same is true of any sales business. If you don't ask for the sale, you won't get it.

Being successful in sales involves getting out there, and meeting lots and lots and lots of people. You have to be completely systematic, and utterly consistent about doing this. If you take these steps, it will help you earn people's trust.

If you follow these tips for face to face sales, you will improve your odds of success. Business is 1% inspiration and 99 % perspiration, and just sticking with it.

Delight Your Clients With Every Project

Keeping your current clients is way easier than getting new clients… so ensuring your clients are happy with your service is very important for retention. Go above and beyond to please your clients so they keep coming back to you for years.

5 Ways to Keep Your Current Clients Happy

1. **ASK QUESTIONS – BEFORE AND DURING THE PROJECT.** Make sure you're asking questions about your new project, both before and during the work. Don't be afraid to ask questions instead of making assumptions; asking questions will help to ensure the work is being done to the client's expectations. Just as important as asking these questions is listening to their answers, and implementing solutions accurately. Most customers want exactly what they expect the first time around, and will not allow for mistakes or do-overs. Ask lots of questions to ensure you know EXACTLY what your clients wants and the results they expect.

2. **COMMUNICATE WITH CONVICTION.** As they say, sometimes it's not what you say, but how you say it. This can be especially true when working with clients. Focus on positive, clear and concise communication. Say what you mean and mean what you say… but be aware of your tone, especially in emails and text messages. Sometimes things can be misread and the meaning misconstrued. Double check your messages before sending them, and add as much detail as possible to eliminate confusion. For example, maybe you can't work on a project after 6pm on Mondays and Wednesdays. Instead, say you CAN work until 6pm on Mondays and Wednesdays and any other time on Tuesdays, Thursdays and Fridays. Then ask how this works for their

project timeline. Not using a tiny contraction in your communications with your clients may seem like something very insignificant, but it changes the way a customer views you from someone that can't get something done to someone that does – as someone that can make things happen in a positive way.

3. **DELIVER THE PROJECT AS PROMISED, AND THEN SOME.** In a vast majority of projects or with most clients, all you need to do is follow through with the project or work as discussed, and on time, to make them happy. If you're looking to exceed their expectations, however, you'll want to go above and beyond. For example, this could be by doing more words in a blog post, creating your own graphics, giving more hours for the same cost, or turning the project in days ahead of deadline. This will make your client feel that you are worth every penny they invested in you and more, and will keep them coming back.

4. **DON'T FORGET TO FOLLOW UP.** No matter which business you enter into, you'll learn the truth to the phrase, "The fortune is in the follow-up." If you want a one-time sale, that's fine, but it's the return customers that will keep you in business. Clients that keep you on for recurring projects, or return over and over again to use your services or goods, are how you're going to make the most money at your freelancing or small business, so be sure you're following up with each client after the work is completed. Following up can be as easy as a quick email or phone call to check in on how they feel about your product or service. You can make sure nothing was missing or wrong, then be sure to mention what other products or services you provide in case they find a need for your services again. The simple email or phone call will give them a reminder of how happy you made them before, and to hire you again.

5. **KEEP IN TOUCH.** Just as in friendships and other relationships, staying in touch with your clients is an essential part of repeat customer work. You'll be the one that does this while many other freelancers or business will not take two minutes to send an email just to say hello, leave a friendly voicemail after hours, or send a Christmas card. This really shows how appreciated your client is and will remind them that even when you're not working for them, they are still important to you and your business.

What other ways do you go above and beyond with your customers?

What's your Competitive Advantage?

Do you know what makes you different from the many other companies or individuals out there who do exactly what you do? What makes you better? What competitive advantage does your business have? Why should someone choose to do business with you? What are your distinguishing points that make you stand out from everyone else in your own unique way?

Mine is that I'm an MBA from a top tier university, I have several companies of my own, and I have a very solid history with entrepreneurship. I know about business and about entrepreneurship because I've lived it on my own. I don't just tell you how to do things, I show you how to do them. I know what works and what doesn't work, and I can save you time, and money, while helping you make MORE money.

You need to talk about what your value proposition is for your client. Your job is to fix a problem that they have. What problems can you fix? I hire people all the time who do word-smithing for me for sales pages, and who do graphics, accounting, and other services, because those aren't my skills. I can write well enough (as evidenced by writing so many blog posts, and books, and other things), but when it comes to the sales side for creating sales pages - that isn't my forte. I know where my limits are, and I'm not an expert in absolutely everything.

TRY THIS EXERCISE...

Write down 20 things that make you unique or different. List what you do, your experiences, your background, and what makes you and your company special.

What is your story? What is your WHY of your business?

What things do you see on that list? Which of those things can you use to help a client solve their problems? What things set you apart?

Once you stop to reflect and meditate on the things that make you different, you can start to understand your unique value proposition for your clients, and be able to offer them better insight into exactly what you can do for them.

DEALING WITH ADVERSITY

Handling Adversity

The reality is that everyone you meet is going through something, or has gone through adversity of some kind. The devil is in how they hey handle adversity when it does strike. It's not so much about completely avoiding problems, and never having them, but rather how you deal with them when they do happen. Because let's face it, stuff happens. If you're like me, it happens far too often for comfort sometimes.

Many acquaintances of mine assume that nothing bad ever happens to me. Actually, that couldn't be further from the truth. I've had melanoma twice. The second time, I caught it sooner than the first, so it was in situ (that means it hadn't spread). I've had to deal with a child who was born 3 months early and had a lot of hurdles to overcome. I was on bed rest for 6 months with the next pregnancy, and 2 months for the third pregnancy. My mom was diagnosed with Multiple Sclerosis when I was only about 13 years old, and I became one of her primary caregivers. In fact, my dad used to leave on business trips for up to a month at a time, even when I was that age, and I was responsible for cooking, grocery shopping, and even paying the family's bills, because there was no such thing as automatic bill pay in those days. I've known adversity. The question is, how did I handle it?

The deal with adversity is that everyone faces some problem or another. To each of us, it is, in biblical terms, our own cross to bear. What defines us and sets us apart is how we bear that cross, and how we handle the adversity which is placed in our way. Do you choose to let it take over your life, or do you deal with it and move on? Do you ever just want to crawl up into a ball, and ignore life? Or do you pull out your big girl pants and just deal with it? I get that some people have mental health issues, and may deal with depression. In their case, seeking medical attention and taking medication may require great courage, and may be what they need to do to handle adversity. Not everyone's problems are the same.

How do you deal with adversity? Does it fire you up, and make you want to fight and win? Or do you run away? Do you pick your battles, and decide what's worth fighting for and what might be worth shouting about? Everyone handles it differently, but it does speak volumes about who we are as people, and how we value ourselves.

Leaders embrace adversity, because they know that it is how they handle that adversity which sets them apart from the crowd. They don't shy away from problems because they are uncomfortable to deal with. Neither do they just rip people to shreds. They face adversity head-on, with kindness, and with skill. That is the mark of a true leader, and someone worth following.

When Everything Sucks

If you're an entrepreneur, you've probably had those times where everything sucks. The sun sucks, your family sucks, the job sucks, clients suck, there's not enough money, so that sucks too. Everything sucks, and you're down in the dumps. Yuck! Blech!

It's no fun when everything hits all at once, because you're the person who everyone else is looking at to be the cheerleader, and the one in charge, making all the decisions. Did I mention that it sucks?

What are some things you can do when everything looks like a miserable, abject, utter failure?

11 Free or Cheap Ways to Get Out Of The Dumps

1. **CALL A FRIEND.** Call a dear friend and meet with them. Sometimes you just need to be around a familiar face. Lunch with my best friend is always a pick-me-up, and I make a point of going out to lunch with her at least once a week. It doesn't matter how much I like the other people in my life, spending time around my best friend is a treat to myself, and a way to take care of myself.

2. **PET YOUR CAT OR DOG.** I pick up the cat who likes to be picked up and petted, and just the action of stroking his silky fur will calm me down dramatically. This also releases endorphins, and releases a lot of tension. Strangely, things always look better after interacting with my cat.

3. **GO FOR A WALK OR GET SOME EXERCISE.** Exercise releases endorphins, and will help reduce your stress level. Getting a little bit of distance from your troubles also helps.

4. **GET SOME SLEEP.** Sometimes I burn the candle at both ends (Okay, a little more often than sometimes). Getting some sleep helps tremendously. When you're tired, you're more likely to be angry and weepy.

5. **TAKE A LONG BATH.** The warm water is soothing. Throw in some Epsom salts (found at any drug store) to help soften your skin, and for added relaxation. Take the time when you get out of the tub to rub in some lovely moisturizer. You'll be amazed at how much better you feel.

6. **TAKE A DAY OFF.** It is OK to take a day off every once in a while. In fact, it's desirable to take a day off every week. There have been studies that show that the human mind and body needs to have one day a week off.

7. **JUMP YOUR SIGNIFICANT OTHER.** It releases lots of endorphins and is an easy way to blow off some steam. Enough said.

8. **KEEP IN MIND THAT THIS TOO SHALL PASS.** Sometimes you just have to remind yourself that whatever it is that is setting you off will pass, and is not permanent.

9. **READ SCRIPTURE OR AFFIRMATIONS.** No matter what your religion is, read some scripture, affirmations, or uplifting reading.

10. **MEDITATE.** Sometimes the simple act of closing your eyes and breathing, and taking a few minutes to just be and exist will really help you deal with whatever it is that is setting you off.

11. **PRACTICE EFT.** Check out some YouTube videos on EFT (Emotional Freedom Techniques), also known as Energy Tapping. This is a very simple way to release whatever blocks have you going in circles, and to deal with anger, disappointment, or other issues. Quite simply, you state that despite the fact that whatever is going wrong is going wrong, you deeply and completely love yourself, while tapping, one hand to the other. There are some more complex variations of this as well.

There are many ways to deal with stress, and to cope with those blah days when nothing is going well at work. Turn those suck-y days around, and deal with them, and you will emerge better at the end of it all.

The Good, The Bad, and The Ugly of Being an Entrepreneur

A lot of times when people hear that I'm an entrepreneur, they start making assumptions about what I'm like, or about what my work ethic must be. Other entrepreneurs get what we go through -- the ups, and the downs, and the sheer unpredictability of being an entrepreneur.

The Good

- Since you are your own boss, it means that you are in control of your destiny. Nobody is telling you what to do, or how to do it. It is quite liberating, but it can be scary at times.
- You get to choose how many hours you're going to work, and when you are going to work. If you want to come into work late, and leave early, no-one is going to notice.
- You get to decide nearly everything about your work. What freedom!
- The money you're making is for yourself, and not some huge corporation.
- You'll be creating jobs and putting money back into the economy. Most job creation actually comes from small businesses.

The Bad

- No-one is there to tell you "no" unless you make a point of surrounding yourself with people who are able to tell you "no".
- It can be terribly easy to go off into the weeds and get lost, and it can be incredibly tempting to just take days off, and to lose focus on what you are trying to accomplish for your business at any given point in time.
- Sometimes you may forget to take care of yourself.

The Ugly

- All decisions are ultimately your own, and the consequences are as well. It's not like when you work for a large corporation where there is plenty of blame to go around. If things don't work out, it's no-one else's fault but your own.

- The unpredictability can be frightening at times. Some days are really good, and some days are really not so good. When clients are misbehaving, complaining, and not paying, it's all yours.

- Income can vary widely, and be all over the place. Some months will be really, really good, and others won't be nearly as good. That means that when planning for expenses and income, you will have to be incredibly conservative so that you know you can survive the lean months.

- If you don't take care of yourself, there won't be a business. So you MUST make time to take care of yourself, which sounds far easier than it actually is.

There are lots of highs and lows of being an entrepreneur, but I think that for me, the benefits far outweigh the costs. I have found that if I have an evening where I need to go take care of my child, then I can do so, and nobody is going to judge me for being less of a mother, or less of an entrepreneur for taking care of my children. The same cannot be said for a corporate position.

Leaders Cry Too

In 2013, I cried more than in the previous 20 years before, and the years since. It was a really rough year, between the death of my father, the death of my aunt, and the death of my beloved kitty of over 21 years. It was, from my perspective, my most horrible year. Life isn't always rainbows and roses. Sometimes life really sucks.

It's okay that it sucks, because life has ups and downs, and death is a natural part of life, and so is grieving. My family got to see me cry, and I cried with them over our losses that year. I cried with my cousins over the loss of their mother. It's important to let people know that it's OK to cry and to grieve. Why shouldn't it be? Leaders cry too. That they cry is especially at important times, and not because they are weak, but maybe because they are strong. Leaders are not afraid of being perceived as weak for being human. It's a condition that affects all of us. By being vulnerable, you are being human, and showing others that it's OK.

What I learned is that you have to take the time to take care of yourself, allow yourself to remember a loved one, and grieve the very real loss that you've experienced. Burying it doesn't do any good, as issues will resurface later. Sometimes those issues will resurface years and years later, so it's best to acknowledge your grief, and loss, and give it a good cry when you need to. Give yourself permission to just be. It's OK.

As I approached my first Christmas without either of my parents, I was struck by how desolate I felt. I was struck by how a piece of me was truly missing. I felt like an orphan, even though I was an adult, with children of my own. That's grief for you. It's not that I grieved all the time. I did celebrate plenty of things, but I also gave myself permission to stop and remember. Leaders cry too sometimes.

TAKE CARE OF YOURSELF

Take Care of Yourself to Take Care of Business

The hardest thing to do when you're an entrepreneur is to take care of yourself. It's true. If you're anything like me, there are kids that need stuff, and they need to be driven somewhere. They also like to eat on a regular basis, have clean clothes to wear, and little things like that. You may or may not have another job, a spouse, and lots of people and things pulling in different directions.

Add everything up, and it can be a serious challenge to get a shower every day, and actually take care of yourself. I know, I've been there, and that is my world every day. I have to trade off 15 more minutes of sleep versus putting on makeup most days of the week. The sleep usually wins out.

You have to take time where you can, and learn to say no to things that aren't as important. Self care needs to become an integral part of your daily habits and rituals. It will help you be able to cope with the long, slow, slog that is being an entrepreneur, and all of the inevitable ups and downs that come with it.

Sometimes you can make small changes that don't take much time that allow you take better care of yourself. That means you'll be able to do a better job and focus better on your business.

They can be tiny changes, like drinking water. Feel like keeping up with a water cup is a pain? Then buy bottled water, and drink that. Increase water consumption, and you will likely feel better. Bonus - your skin and hair will thank you as well. Double bonus - if your feet are prone to swelling, staying hydrated may help with that as well.

Schedule a few minutes a day when you can exercise. It doesn't have to be a 2 hour production. You can do stretches by your desk when you take a break every hour. It will make you more productive. And you will feel better because you'll be giving your body the attention and movement that it needs.

Package healthy snacks, so you won't be tempted to eat junk food. That can be as simple as bringing an apple to work, or keeping some apples at work. OR, you can buy bagged apples and eat those instead. If you don't like apples, how about bagged carrots? The key here is to go simple, and find ways to you set yourself up for success.

My favorite way to get some "me time" is to take a hot bath - and shut the door. I can usually manage to keep the kids out of the bathroom, if I sneak into the bathroom quietly, and shut the door.

Saying, "No" to things that aren't as important to you is also crucial. For me, those things are going to be different than they are for you, however in my house I'm not the best cook, and I've been permanently banned from using the washing machine. (I managed to dye all the clothes in the house pink within the first month of our marriage. I have some serious talent!) I choose to farm out the things that don't mean as much to me so that I can keep my sanity. Hiring a maid or yard maintenance company is a quick and easy way to offload some chores.

Another easy way to offload, which requires some diligence on your part, but that will pay off handsomely in the end, is to train your children and spouse to help around the house. If there are other people in the house, they should be doing their fair share of the chores on a regular basis, and they should be doing them well. Kids can help with unloading and reloading the dishwasher, scrubbing toilets, taking out the trash, vacuuming the floors, dusting, and more. You may have to insist on them repeating a chore if they fail to do it correctly, but if you persist, you will have a huge amount of help and labor in your house.

As much as I've tried to come up with a way to get more hours in a day, I'm still bound by the space-time continuum. There are only 24 hours for me too. Yet- I manage to get the things that are most important to me done, with flourish and style. The things that are less important slide, and may not get done.

You must make self-care a regular part of your regimen. That means picking your favorite means of self care, and following through with those on a regular basis.

In order to take care of your business, your family and your life, you have to take care of yourself first. You have to make sure that your health is not only a focus, but a priority. Make sure that you're getting the help you need so that you can do the things you want to do.

Staying Focused

Projects can be extremely easy to start. Following through and keeping focus can be extremely difficult, no matter what the project is. In my life, the project was starting two new businesses concurrently. Also, when it's Girl Scout Cookie season, it's crazy in my house. For my daughter one season, her goal was selling over 2000 boxes of Girl Scout Cookies. At the same time she was working on getting to the Gold Level in Gymnastics for the next year. I was also nudging her towards doing some tournaments on the NASKA circuit (a very competitive Karate Circuit). All of these things take time, perseverance, and keeping focus.

The path to success is really not smooth in any way. In fact, it's pretty bumpy, and some of the potholes could hold an elephant. In order to succeed, you have to work on keeping focus, and sticking with it even when things get really hard. Some days are really dark, and nothing seems to go right. In the case of starting a new business, there are lots of potholes, and sometimes they have rattlesnakes in them. The key is to keep at it, and work on keeping focus. It can be done.

It's a lot like _The Little Engine That Could_ – keep telling yourself, "I think I can, I think I can". Eventually you will get there, and you will have a successful business. Or, in the case of my daughter, she will have sold over 2000 boxes of cookies, or 3000, or whatever her goal was - because she kept chipping away at the problem until it went away. She actually sold 6115 boxes of cookies that year, and 3000 the next. She reached her goals in Gymnastics. She also started competing in NASKA, and has been steadily improving in the rankings since she started.

Most achievements in life are like that. They are a question of having a good idea, and sticking with it and keeping focus. Some achievements are pure luck, and a few others are brilliance. I'm not arguing that creativity, brilliance and luck don't also play a role, but you'll never get to experience those if you don't keep your nose to the grindstone.

Increase Your Business Success with The Power of Positive Thinking

It's no secret that with entrepreneurship brings huge amounts of stress, but learning to maintain a positive business outlook can be a learned skill. It will help to stay upbeat, productive, and help keep order and balance in life.

Here are the best ways to maintain, and even increase, a positive attitude to multiply success in your life and business.

- **GIVE.** Negativity can be caused by concentrating on what you think are negative parts of your life… or by focusing on what you DON'T have. You can immediately change your negativity by giving to others and sharing your skills with the people around you. Helping others always creates positive emotions, and forces you to focus on others, rather than on yourself and what you think you're lacking. Never hesitate or doubt your value. Even the smallest of gestures you share can cause a massive change in another's perspective and attitude, and when you see what a difference you can make in others, you will feel better and more positive about yourself.

- **SHOW APPRECIATION.** One of the easiest ways to increase your positivity is to express appreciation. Showing thankfulness for what you already have will let go of any negativity that you may be holding on to. Gratitude immediately puts you in the feeling of love, and wherever love resides, fear and other negative emotions cannot. The most effortless ways to put more gratitude in your life is to show it every morning. When you wake up, tell yourself at least 5 things you are thankful for – it can be spoken aloud or in your head, but they must be detailed and come from the heart. Close your eyes and feel it in your body and mind; think of how grateful you are for all that you have, and all that has happened to you. The feeling of positivity and happiness immediately upon waking is the perfect way to start your day, and will make your day more successful and far less stressful.

- **IMAGINE YOUR SUCCESS.** Many of the world's greatest and richest people use the power of attraction and visualization to magnetize toward them everything they want in their lives. To use the power of attraction, just close your eyes and think of a positive event that has happened before. Think of it exactly as it happened, and place yourself within it. Feel the emotions you felt when this positive event occurred. Keep yourself in this positive feeling and imagine your day and events of your day going exactly the same way – they go exactly as you want, with yes-es and positivity throughout your day. When you have a particularly important event or meeting, use this method to prepare your power for the attraction of positivity.

- **CONTROL YOUR BREATHING.** There is a common belief that those who can control their breathing can control their lives, and the more balance you have in your breath, the more balance you'll find in your life. Think back to a time when you felt you lost control of a situation – What happened to your breathing pattern? Your anxiety or anger caused your breathing to become quickened and shortened. Once you learn to control your breathing, then you will better understand the effect it has on your emotions, both positive and negative. To learn better breath control, escape to a quiet space. Take a breath in through your nose and feel the air enter your body and go deep into your lungs. As soon as it hits the deepest parts of your lungs, breathe out through your mouth to release all the tension.

By controlling what you're thinking, and how you're reacting to a situation, you will find that you have much more control over the outcomes than you ever thought possible.

Embrace Fear and Negativity in Your Business

Whether you're still debating about starting your own business, or you're already established, two of the most common causes of a stalled growth are negativity and fear. Negative thoughts can come from a likely deeper fear of failure, and sometimes, even a fear of success. Instead of letting your thoughts become your future, embrace your fear and use it as fuel to keep moving toward your goals.

3 Tips For Moving Past Fear and Negativity

1. **NAME YOUR FEARS.** Naming your fears takes the internal negativity and puts it outside of yourself. It also helps to make it seem less serious. This is much like when someone has a chronic illness. You start by recognizing that you are not your illness. You are someone with a chronic illness. For example, I'm Haley with migraines, not the lady with migraines. You are not your fears. You are someone with fears. Overcoming them will be much easier when you realize that you are not defined by your fears, illnesses or anything else for that matter.

2. **JOURNAL.** Journaling is a huge part of overcoming any emotional setback, but especially so in conquering fear. Buy yourself a journal or notebook that you can dedicate to Negativity Notes, or something similar. Make it pretty, and buy a nice pen to go with it if it will help motivate you to write in it.

   When your negative thoughts make their appearance, write them down EVERY TIME. Once you collect enough Negativity Notes, you'll get a better understanding on what is going on in your head, and when. Likely it's been thoughts you've had before, and they repeat frequently. This clarity will help you to avoid situations when you have your negative thoughts and fears.

Be sure to keep track of your wins and revelations. This will help you track your progress. Being able to look back on fears you had, and how you overcame them and the good that results, will help keep you encouraged during hard times.

3. **FACE YOUR FEARS.** It may seem scary, but facing your fears head on helps you move through them. We all need to step out of our comfort zones, but when we are faced with our fears head on, it's painful. We naturally want to avoid any type of pain. When we face our fears and show them who's boss of our lives, the pain will shrink and eventually disappear. However, if you decide to stay in your comfort zone to avoid pain, the fear will continue to fester and grow stronger. Fears don't disappear when we ignore them. Use this fear as an opportunity to grow and become empowered. There are many fears you will experience while owning your own business, accept that, and don't quit.

As once said by George Addair, "Everything you've ever wanted is on the other side of fear." Once you accept and move through your fear, you will get everything you want. By implementing my tips to do so, you're only 3 steps away from finally reaching your dreams!

Follow Your Heart

As I moved towards starting Extension of You Home Care, one of the things that we were looking for in employees for our company was passion. We were looking for passion to provide care in ways never seen before, with a different business model than your typical home care company. We were looking for the best of the best in sales, caregivers, office managers, care managers, and everyone we work with. Note, that I didn't say that I was looking for people who have the most qualifications, or the deepest work history. What we were looking for was **heart**. We wanted, and still want, people who are delighted to do this work, with all their heart and soul.

From a personal perspective, it's also important to follow your heart. If you aren't into something, for whatever reason, your performance will suffer. Yes, there are times when you just do what you have to do, because that is what a job is. At the end of the day though, there has to be a spark, some love, and wanting to do this job, or you will not do very well.

It is why I started the company - I feel passionately about it, and am so excited to get up every morning. I want to hire more people like me. People who are passionate, and love doing this, and feel called to this type of job. I want people to follow their hearts.

What are your passions? Do you follow them? Do you follow your heart?

Give Yourself

To be an effective leader, you must have people's trust. In order to gain that trust, you quite simply are going to have to give yourself to them. Being a leader is about confidence that people have in you. They have to trust that your decisions are going to be in their interest. After all, most people care about causes, but they also really care about themselves.

Okay - so how do you start? I think that leadership is about influence, but also about serving. It is much easier to influence others if you give back. Think about it.

Who would you be most willing to help? Someone who has made a lot of deposits in your bank, or someone who hasn't? If someone only takes, then how quickly and happily are you going to respond to their requests? What if they did simple things for you – like thanking you for tasks done? Or remembered to ask about your kids, or your family?

Leadership isn't about managing people. It's about influencing, mentoring and getting other people to see your vision and follow your direction. It's actually more difficult to effectively lead people than it is to manage them. A manager will tell people how and when to show up, and exactly what to do. A leader will influence them to think for themselves, own the problem, and solve it.

By leading people, you must give of yourself, and give people permission to do their best.

Think of leadership as relationship building. How would you go about building relationships with people so that they will trust you? I think that it's easy if you give yourself. You will receive back, multiple-fold.

Respect Yourself

After I wrote about people you should respect, my oldest daughter reminded me that I had forgotten someone very important. She is correct. The most important person to respect is yourself. You can't do anyone else any good if you do not respect yourself.

Here are some tips on how to respect yourself:

1. Accept that there are only 24 hours in a day. Only so much can get done. Understand those limits, and respect them. Don't beat yourself up for being just one person.

2. You have to sleep, eat right and exercise. These are basic tips, but are so important, because you can't do much else unless you are taking care of yourself.

3. Give yourself permission to be less than perfect. People make mistakes. They forget, and they get lost. Be kind do yourself, and cut yourself some slack.

I have to agree with my daughter - and give her a ton of points for pointing out that the most important person to respect is yourself. Sometimes we learn a lot from our kids. I've heard it said that if you don't take care of yourself, there won't be a business. Because without you, there is no business. I guess she had it right after all.

Let Go

"We must let go of the lives we have planned for ourselves so as to have the life that is planned for us".

Truthfully, no matter how much you plan, things don't always work out according to plan. Layoffs happen. People get sick. People sometimes die. Sometimes it's best to let go, and pick yourself up and keep going. There have been a number of times in my life when things went seriously wrong, and against my plan. Sometimes, it's little things, like the road I'm needing to get on being blocked, and having to make a detour.

It can be incredibly difficult to accept that perhaps there is another plan for us in life. Whether you believe in fate, God's plan, or just picking yourself up. Sometimes you just have to accept, and keep on going.

One of the questions I ask myself when people irritate or annoy me is whether it's worth reacting over. Usually the answer that comes back to me is a very simple, "No". They aren't worth the energy; they aren't worth the time to put a line in the sand.

If you think about it in terms of energy, the decision to let go can be easier. You only have so much energy, and you get to decide how you're going to spend that energy. Are you going to spend your energy fighting things that can't or won't be changed, or are you going to spend your energy focusing on the things that will be changed, and where you will have the most influence. Do you want to spend your energy fighting and creating negative vibes, or are you going to focus it in a positive direction?

Listen to Your Heart, for your Business' Sake

So many times in business we do things that don't feel right - because we don't listen to our heart or conscience. The cool thing about being a business owner is that you get to listen to your heart, and to take your business in the direction that your heart wants you to go. I think that it is critically important to listen to that inner voice when making critical business decisions.

I've found when I didn't listen to my heart, and instead ignored it, I ended up making the wrong decision. Obviously, in business you have to have numbers, and focus on numbers, however, there is a fairly large amount of intuition that goes along with being an entrepreneur, and you have to make calculated risks, and decide what you're going to do based on those risks.

Sometimes we make decisions that feel "icky" in business. If something feels bad, then don't do it. Because if you make decisions in your business that are counter to your feelings and intuition, you are going to feel uncomfortable about them. And after all, if you own a business, it is your heart and soul, and where you are focusing most of your energy. You'll be giving yourself lots of icky vibes.

Or... you can listen to your inner vibe, and make sure that your business decisions are made in a way that you feel comfortable, and are in tune with. You'll be happier, and you will do better in your business because you'll have a vibe that you're happy with.

Staying Motivated Through a Long, Cold Winter

After the holidays are over, winter starts to drag on. The cold makes you want to just curl up under a blanket, and the short days of hardly any daylight make you sleepy. Winter takes a toll on everyone's mood and motivation, which can be especially difficult while running a business. You'd be surprised to discover that winter can be one of the most productive times of the year if you know where and how to focus your energy.

Whether you own a business or just a blog, here are some tips to keep your business and your enthusiasm for its operation continuously running at its very best during these long winter months.

- **STAY ON A SCHEDULE.** Make sure you're going to bed and getting up at the same time every day. Once you're in bed, do not open your phone or check emails. Check out for the day and go to sleep. Before you go to sleep, however, make sure you're set for the day ahead by creating a to-do list. This will keep you from laying in bed awake, running all of tomorrow's tasks through your mind. If you work from home, it will make you feel better to get up and shower, get dressed, and get ready as if you were going to an office environment. It helps to wake you up and get your brain ready for the day ahead.

- **SET ATTAINABLE GOALS.** Make a list of tasks for both short term and long term goals. Like to-do lists, creating a list of small goals to help you reach each of the items on the list will help maintain productivity and your motivation in your current projects.

  Already feeling worn out? Start small. If you feel you won't ever finish a specific item on your list by the end of the day, choose a small, more attainable goal to feel less overwhelmed. Once you complete the goal, this little win will help keep you motivated and ready to manage larger tasks at hand.

- **CELEBRATE SUCCESSES.** Using positive reinforcement, even on yourself, can be reassuring and motivating during dreary winter weather. Reward yourself for a job well done (or even competed at all)! This can be simple, like a cup of coffee or a short phone call with a friend. If your accomplishment is much larger, treat yourself to a spa day or a new pair of shoes. Knowing these special treats are within arm's reach will help keep you moving toward the finish line.

- **GET OUT AND NETWORK.** Sitting in the office gets old and can add to the winter blues. Get out and network. Engaging in conversation, having a great meal and just being surrounded by new scenery will help rejuvenate your spirit and get you raring to go again.

- **CREATE A MORE ENJOYABLE WORK ENVIRONMENT.** You'll be shocked by how much more work you can get done when you've got a comfortable, inspiring workspace. Reorganize your office, rearrange your desk, add a few family pictures in frames or trinkets on the walls, as well as some inspiration quotes. Create an office environment that screams positivity — your attitude about your business shows in your work, and having the right attitude can start in the very office in which you sit down to work.

The Groundhog Day Effect

We've all felt it. That strange déjà vu sensation; the feeling that you've been in the same spot or done the same thing before. It's almost like an out-of-body or sixth sense experience. This is the same idea behind what people call the, "Groundhog Day Effect" – doing the same thing over and over again for your business and within your life and simply getting nowhere.

Whether it is the same meetings or the same scheduled family time every week, being stuck in a routine can feel comfortable and predictable, but at the same time, it can restrict your business and personal growth. If you find this is happening to you and your business, you're not alone. Luckily this can be changed with just a few simple strategies to get out of your Groundhog Day spiral.

To get out of this spiral, you must regain passion – both personally and for your business – and this can be as easy as following these 4 effective tactics.

1. **START SMALL.** Don't change every part of your business and your life at one time. It can be overwhelming and can cause more harm than good. For changes in life and business, do a little at a time and slowly. The best way to do this is to think of everything that's stuck in a rut and write it down in a place you see every day. Start with either the most meaningful change for your life or your company, or start with the easiest change. As you go along, you may need to make other changes to modify part of your list. Don't be surprised if you add more to your list as you go along – this will keep you from returning to your Groundhog Day life.

2. **GET OUT OF THE OFFICE.** Sometimes just going somewhere new to do your work or grab your morning coffee can refresh your mind. Getting a new literal view can give you a new figurative view of both your professional and personal life. This may be something to do every day, but make it spontaneous! Planned outings become part of the cycle of the Groundhog Day Effect.

3. **GET UNCOMFORTABLE.** It's only natural to feel uneasy when facing change in any facet of our lives. To really get out of your rut, you must accept that feeling discomfort is normal, but it's also necessary to get back on track. Whether it's starting to make cold phone calls or applying to participate in an event, you have to get uncomfortable before anything will get better. Once you start doing more and more awkward things, the less nervous you'll become with the next one.

4. **FIND A NEW HOBBY.** Or you can pick back up an old one. Being in a rut professionally can be caused by boredom in your personal life. Find something fun that you love to do, and actually DO IT. Don't just pick up yoga as a new activity, and then do it only for a week, or because you feel like you have to. Do your new hobby or activity because you deserve to have a fun and entertaining life besides running a business. Plus, worries and anxiety tend to be pushed aside while you're doing something you enjoy.

Have you ever found yourself in a déjà vu or 'Groundhog Day Effected' life? How did you find your way out of your rut?

Expand Your Influence and Make The World a Better Place

In the last couple of years, I started challenging myself to really expand my influence and make a difference in the world. I have long been a Girl Scout Leader, and after many years in that capacity, I wanted to do MORE. So, I started really working with the kids to identify great community service projects. Then I started looking at what I was doing with my career, and where I was going. Some of that was a natural part of getting my MBA, and some of it had to do with seeing my parents aging, and dying. Tough times, to be sure, but what was I going to do with myself. So, I decided to see about expanding my influence, and making the world a better place.

I started looking at what skills I possess, and which skills I do not possess in abundance, and decided on a business venture which showcases my strengths. I hired people, and found a great partner who is strong where I am weak, so it is a great match. I also wanted to do business a bit differently than had been done before. We decided to start a home care business, in addition to the Care Patrol Franchise we bought. We wanted to pay people a little bit better, and actually offer benefits. Treat people how they deserve to be treated. Make them feel cherished. That goes for both our clients and our caregivers. We also encourage our employees to improve themselves, and get a higher level of education, and more skills, so that they can work themselves into a better career track. This also allows them to make more money than before, and hopefully raise themselves out of poverty, and improves the middle class. It's just my way of expanding my influence and making the world a better place.

Why do this? Quite simply, why not? Find people who will work with me, and work hard. Treat them well, and they will treat you well. I don't need to extract every single dollar out of them, because I realize that part of the way to get the business to grow is by word of mouth. We will get more clients, and more caregivers if we do the right things. It also means that I'll be able to go to sleep at night, knowing that I did the right thing. In the end, it's between God and me, and I realize that is important too.

But seriously, why not try to expand your influence and make the world a better place? Why wouldn't you? Why not step up, and make a difference? No matter how small, you have to start somewhere. Otherwise, aren't you just existing? What's the point in that?

Challenge: Support Your Local Businesses

I have a challenge for everyone who reads this: Support your local businesses, especially the small ones. I make a point of bringing business to local businesses for a variety of reasons. As we start gearing up for the holidays, why not buy local gifts? Support your local small businesses!

3 Reasons to Support your Local Businesses

1. You are putting money back into your local economy. Your hard-earned money will go straight into the pocket of someone local, and they will be able to raise their families, take them to local restaurants, and generally fuel the local economy.

2. You are frequently getting products of a better quality. My local travel agent is amazing and provides personalized service. My favorite chocolate shop produces a product that is, quite simply, superior to mass-produced products.

3. You are creating local jobs. In addition to the business owners, if you help the business by supporting it regularly, the business will likely grow. That may mean more jobs. Which means lower unemployment.

My Favorite Local Businesses in the Triangle area of North Carolina

- Escazu Chocolates produce some of the most amazing chocolates from bean to bar. The quality of the product is impossible to beat, and the cost is very attractive as well.

- DWB Vacations is my preferred travel agent. I've thrown some insane requests at Crystal, and she's come through every time. Cruise for 17 at Christmas time on short notice? Oh yes, we also need a handicapped accessible stateroom! She came through with flying colors every single time.

- <u>Second Empire Restaurant</u> is a lovely fine dining restaurant. The menu varies seasonally. I could go just for the cheese and the desserts though.

- <u>Dos Taquitos</u> is my favorite Mexican food joint. There are all sorts of interesting things hanging from the ceiling, and the decor has to be seen to be believed. To say it is eclectic would be putting it mildly.

- <u>The Jewel Smith</u> is an iconic local jeweler near Duke. Their jewelry is handcrafted and beautiful. They also consistently win a ton of awards.

- <u>Stonehaven</u> is another small, local jeweler. Ron has won a number of prestigious awards for his designs.

- <u>The Wine Merchant</u> is a small local vintner. They have some great choices, including "Josh" which is a lovely, inexpensive Cab. They have some great high-end choices too, so just work your way on through.

If you look around, you will find lots of small, local businesses in your area. When you support those small businesses, you are helping a family send their child to ballet classes, not putting money into the deep pockets of a large corporation.

I've seen some interesting statistics about how much impact support of small, local businesses has on the local economy, and it is staggering. I like to think that a huge percentage of every dollar I'm paying to a local business is staying here locally. That means that I'm making the area around me, my community, a better place. What's not to like?

Why not try a local business, and support the local economy while you're at it? What are your favorite local businesses? How do you support your local businesses?

Apply Your Skills

Do you apply your skills? Do you know when to use them, and when to lay low? It has been a long time coming for me to learn when to use them, and when to lay low.

When my younger daughter was in seventh grade, it was probably the first time she had to study, and it was quite the eye-opening experience. I think that it was also the first time she had to really advocate for herself in school. Learning to advocate for yourself is really a tough skill to learn, but if anyone should have that skill, this kid should. After all, she's the one who will argue with customers who tell her no during cookie season. If you tell her you're on a diet, she'll tell you to buy anyway, and put the cookies in the freezer for when you go off your diet. It's amazing how successful she is.

She is incredibly successful at selling lots and lots of Girl Scout Cookies. I'd guess that for most people, selling over 3000 boxes in a year is a lot of cookies. This is a kid who will argue with a rock, and win. She considers arguing about things to be a sport. Rules are suggestions only from her perspective. In her mind, rules are meant to be tested.

And yet, she has her struggles. She has run into a couple of situations at school where she needs to advocate for herself, and ask to do make-up work from an absence. She said she asked, but the teacher said, "no". So she quit arguing, and rolled over and cried. Now, it's time for the rubber to hit the road, so to speak. She had to learn when to just bite her tongue and say nothing – such as during the invasion drill at school when some kid was acting up next to her; she waved at him to be quiet, and got into trouble. But she also needs to learn when to use that Agent Weaselburger Style on her teacher, and negotiate what she wants, how she wants. I'm trying to teach her to be persistent about her grades and assignments, because at the end of the day, they are hers to live with.

I spend a lot of time doing this with people who have worked for me as well. I teach people when to push, when not to push. I teach them when to use skills, when to be a leader, and also when to hide. It takes a lot of skill to learn, but ultimately is worth it. If the knowledge I pass along helps just one other person, it will have been put to great use.

What about you? Do you apply your skills? Whether those skills are leadership, negotiation, or advocacy, do you apply them?

MAINTAINING PRODUCTIVE BUSINESS RELATIONSHIPS

Make Deposits to Build Relationships

If you want to build trust, you must first build relationships. To build trusting relationships, and get people to like you, you'll need to start by making deposits with them.

In most cases, people take a while to get to know each other. In a professional environment, you are putting people together who otherwise might never socialize with one another and expecting them to behave like professionals, and actually work together. That means acting like a team, before you've actually gotten to that point in your mind, or your relationship. You had better be able to build those skills up quickly so that you can build those relationships that you're going to need to advance your career, and lead your team, and your group. This is doubly important if you're leading up, or leading within the team, since you're not already in a leadership position.

So what exactly does making deposits mean?

Making deposits can come in many formats, but it means making deposits in your relationship with others before making any withdrawals. In a business environment, making deposits can be with employees, referral sources, or the community at large. If you are working with other entrepreneurs, ask them how you can help them, and what kinds of clients they need or want. Offer to be a problem solver. Don't just ask for referrals, instead, bring them clients, and solve their problems. Remember, you're going to have to make between 7 and 10 deposits for every time you want to make a withdrawal. That's a lot of deposits. You need to make a habit of making those deposits early, and often.

People have to know you to like you. They have to trust you to follow you. Build on that, to become a better leader.

Build Trust

One of the key requirements for leading people effectively is trust. They have to be able to trust your decisions. I would argue that it's probably easier to obtain that trust in your private life, and in volunteer work, than it is in the corporate environment. That's because in your private life and volunteer work, people assume that you are what you say you are, and that there are no hidden agendas. Corporate life is not nearly so forgiving. Even if you are exactly who you say you are, and entirely consistent, some people are loathe to trust, and are constantly looking for those hidden agendas. So, how *do* you build trust?

1. **Do What You Say You Will Do.** If you say you will deliver something at a particular time, then do so. In order for people to believe you about the big stuff, they need to be able to believe you about the little stuff. Deliver what you say you will deliver, on time. Sometimes this is much harder than it seems. It may mean saying "no" because you can't or won't do something, rather than saying "yes" because you feel bad about saying no.

2. **Be Consistent.** This one is hard. You have to be the same person every day. Deliver consistent results every time. If people know you will deliver results every time, they come to trust you. One way I do that is to send out reminder emails for every single Girl Scout meeting. People know that they will get a reminder for every meeting, and I will remind them of the time and location. It costs me a couple of minutes to do, but the parents don't have to rely on their memory, and I get more consistent responses from them as well.

3. **Be Grateful.** Say Thank you. Say thank you early, often and regularly. It costs you nothing, but means so much to the other person. It can be

so hard to remember to be grateful, and to express that gratitude. It is easy to take others for granted. Stop, and say thanks.

Building Trust sounds easy, but can be very hard to do. It is necessary to build that trust in order to lead.

Pay it Forward in Business

Some of my favorite things in life are Random Acts of Kindness, and paying it forward. In this post, I'll talk about ways to pay it forward in the business environment. Why would you want to do such a thing? It boils down to a simple concept that transcends cultures: Karma. I firmly believe that paying it forward in the workplace is one of the keys to being successful.

5 Tips to Pay it Forward in the Workplace

1. Write a thank you note when someone does something nice for you. If they are an employee, send a copy to their supervisor.
2. Do something nice for the most difficult person you work with. Sometimes a bit of kindness goes a long way.
3. Buy coffee or lunch for the person behind you in line, and ask them to pay it forward.
4. Bring in doughnuts or bagels for breakfast for the department, or maybe just cookies one afternoon.
5. Help someone by doing something above and beyond your usual routine, just because you can.

In short, paying it forward, and encouraging others to pay it forward in business is a fun way to contribute to a great work environment. Don't leave it up to only management to set the tone of the office - you can contribute as well. Consider finding new ways to pay it forward..

What ways can you think of to pay it forward?

Maintain a Professional Attitude

Some days, maintaining a professional attitude in business can be very difficult indeed. While it may be temporarily satisfying to tell someone what you really think in the heat of the moment, it is not necessarily in your best interest to do so. Some clients, customers, or employees, really, truly deserve to hear what you're thinking. Sharing those thoughts isn't in your best interest most times, though. That's why I decided to pull together a few tips and reminders.

7 Tips for Maintaining a Professional Attitude

1. Remember - Email, Phone Calls, Voice Mail, and Text Messages are not an instant form of communication and do not have to be answered immediately. There will be times when it is best to craft your answer, and wait 24 hours before sending it. Sometimes cooling down before sending off that email will mean that you avoid making an ass out of yourself.

2. If someone asks you for an answer, ask to think it over, and let them know you will get back to them, within X amount of time. You don't have to agree with everything. You don't have to agree to do everything every time. Coming up with an instant answer isn't necessarily a requirement. There will be times when you are considering a major issue, and it will behoove you to think over that question for a day or two.

3. Bite your tongue. If someone makes an outrageous comment, it may be best to let it slide, and come back to it later, when you're in a calmer frame of mind. Sometimes things are best left alone entirely. There will be some comments that people make in the workplace that are completely inappropriate. In those cases, it may be best to go to their

management or superior rather than going to them directly. Be ready to provide proof for backup in these types of situations.

4. There is absolutely NO place for violence in the workplace. Be careful to maintain that workplace "mask" in place. Do not swing things, or hit your hand with your pen, or otherwise demonstrate aggression physically. Make a point of leaving the situation at the earliest opportunity. Do not engage these types of people. I worked with someone who came into a meeting where we had a disagreement, and he literally sat in the meeting hitting a golf putter against his hand the entire meeting. It didn't help that he was also about 6'4" tall, and 250 lbs. That incident completely destroyed all trust that I had in him, and in his organization. It has been several years since that meeting, and I still remember it quite clearly. That type of behavior has no place in business.

5. Be aware of your body's demands. This means, if you are about to head into a long meeting, and you have not eaten, eat a handful of protein, or bring a snack with you. Avoid sugar lows. Make sure to use the restroom before the meeting starts. Make sure you are well rested. It is much harder to react appropriately to a situation when you are tired, cranky, and otherwise irritable from easily remedied issues. I have long thought that if someone is going to schedule a lunch meeting, they had better be prepared for people to either bring their lunches, or better yet, to provide food.

6. Let some things slide. In today's American Society, there can be the temptation to get HR involved in every single little situation, and consider lawsuits for every infraction, real or imagined. Realize that for every time you make a report to HR, you are creating a reputation for yourself. You must decide if it is worth the cost to your own reputation. I understand that there are certain things that absolutely should be dealt with through HR, and through legal means, but you need to decide which things are worth it. Once you report something, you should be prepared for some amount of backlash, and possibly a reputation in the job market. That could make it harder for you to find a job later, and also, some people may refuse to do business with you altogether, even if you are in the right. That doesn't make it right, but that is how people act sometimes.

7. Remind yourself that many times the offense is in the mind of the person offended. It is possible, and even likely, that absolutely no offense was intended by the other party. Ask yourself if you think that the offense was intentional. I think that in most cases, the answer is an honest "no". Many times stupid things leave our mouths, as we insert our feet into our mouths up to our heels. Before you react, consider whether the other person was just having a stupid moment or whether they were actually trying to cause offense.

Maintaining a professional attitude is mostly about being aware of what's going on and what is really being said. Most of the time, people really are clueless. It never ceases to amaze me how people will say the worst things, not realizing the impact of what they've said. Sometimes they do really stupid things. When my husband or kids do things, I will ask them why they did something in particular, and frequently, I get nothing more than dumb looks. Know that your colleagues and other professionals also do the same thing. They are adults, and probably won't enjoy being called out for doing stupid things though, so you have to be a bit more discreet about it, and sometimes act like nothing happened. Take the high road, and bite your tongue as needed.

Anticipate Needs

Anticipate needs. One of the signs of a leader is the ability to see what needs to be done, then stepping in to take care of it. It's a two step process, and the second part is every bit as important as the first. If you see a problem that needs to be fixed, and don't step in to fix it, that is NOT leadership or anticipation.

The reason I bring this up is that I've noticed in my years of managing people that there are several different kinds of people: 1) Those who notice problems, and fix them. 2) Those who notice problems, and do not fix them. And, 3) Those who don't notice anything, so there is no way they could fix something they didn't see in the first place. It's important to be the first of those types of people.

In the work environment, it's important to establish a leadership position, and one of the easiest ways to do that is to identify meaningful problems, and come up with solutions for them. Work on anticipating needs. Once the solution is identified, then follow through on fixing the problem. If you need additional help or resources, then consider recruiting teammates, depending on the problem, or asking your manager for additional resources. Be prepared to justify your need for resources, and have a very specific set of requests for exactly what you're trying to accomplish.

In short, figure out where you are going, and what you're doing. Figure out what needs to be done next, and do it. It sounds very simple, but is not always as easy as it sounds. Anticipate need - and take care of it.

If you can do this, you will impress everyone around you, and get much further ahead. Of course, you will need to let people know what you did, so that you get proper recognition.

Pick Your Battles

Pick your Battles, carefully, in life and in your career. One of the most difficult lessons in life is learning which battles to fight. You, and only you, can decide how you will expend your energy and time. It can be tough to remember that others do not get to make those decisions for you. Your family, your boss and your children don't get to make these decisions. Only you do.

Remember that any time you are battling, you are using your energy in a particular way. Would you rather use your energy for good and positive things? Or to fight?

One example of this is deciding when to say "no" at work. You always retain the right to say "no" to something you cannot do.

Some good reasons to say no:

- You lack the correct skill set, and cannot quickly gain that set (i.e. this is not a simple stretch)
- An activity is illegal or unethical
- A job is beyond what you can do from a time-management perspective

For now, I will not address the first two, but instead I'll address the third item. If you are asked to perform a job function that you simply do not have the time to perform, it is far better to decline, and explain that you cannot perform it due to time restrictions. Be very prepared to have a current list of your tasks and be ready to negotiate which tasks you should actually be working on. By being willing to negotiate and prioritize your tasks, according to business needs, you will gain your manager's respect and appreciation. We all need to know what our limits are, and recognize that there are only so many hours in a day. Not everything can be done, and compromises have to be reached. Pick your battles.

If we fail to recognize that there are limits to the space-time continuum, it is to our own detriment, and suddenly we find ourselves frazzled, and unable to meet our commitments. It is better to stretch a little, but recognize limits, than to turn into a harried mess or drop commitments, than to simply say 'No'. Simply put, learn to say no, or you will be crunchy and taste good with ketchup. Make sure that you spend your time wisely, and in a way that is consistent with the needs that your business has.

Communication is Key

Communication is the most important skill in the workplace. The classes I've used the most from college are my freshman English classes. Notice that I didn't mention programming, C++, Java, Data Structures, or Networking. I didn't mention accounting, Leadership, or Economics. I said that the class that was the most valuable was plain English. That is because communication is critical. In a lot of ways, communicating, and communicating thoroughly and well, is the most challenging aspect of my work. It is a challenge every single day.

I have to send status, tell people what to do, how to do it, and make sure that clients, customers and employees know what I'm doing. I have to talk to, email with, and communicate with each and every person I work with, make sure that everyone is on the same page, and that there are no mysteries to anyone about what is going on. There is a lot of communication between teams. In order for them to work together, there must be communication at all times.

The ultimate goal is complete transparency. This happens only when there is adequate communication. Communicating effectively means a LOT of communication between the different parties. Making sure that everyone knows what is going on, and communicating that information with everyone is a challenge. I often find myself communicating, and communicating some more. Whether we are using email, instant messaging sessions, status meetings, or text messages, they are all about communications. Those communications require clear, concise descriptions with enough details to tell what is going on, without leaving anything to the imagination, and without overwhelming the recipient with information - a fine line, indeed.

Communication Tip: Ditch Email

If there is one communication tip that I have for people in the modern era, it is that they ditch Email. Why do I say that?

I say that because I think that people rely entirely too much on Email. I know that I have been guilty of it myself. Rather than get up and go find someone, I've sent those emails. You know the kind - asking a question, asking a favor, needing a response. Sitting in my chair, wondering when I'm going to get a response, wasting time. So, my suggestion to you is this - Get up and walk to their desk, and spend some face to face time. Pick up the phone and call. Use other methods of communication, but do not rely solely on email.

Now, I'm not saying that some things aren't well suited to email. Email is not a synchronous form of communication, no matter how much we try to make it so. Sometimes you will encounter people who simply don't read their emails. If they are slack about responding, what are you going to do? You can't expect people to instantly give you the answers you want, when you need them. Get up and go find them, I say. Pick up the phone. Don't rely entirely on electronics to communicate with people.

By spending time face to face, and talking to people, you will be perceived as more caring, more interested, and a better performer. People will respond if you seek them out, and you will get what you need faster. In this day and age, anything that yields faster results, with less work is good. It's a win-win in my book. Try it and see what happens. Get out from behind the desk, and try it out.

What do you think? Would you ditch email?

Negotiate Everything!

Nearly everything in life is negotiable to some extent. As an American Woman, this has been a realization that has been particularly slow to come to me, because I was raised to do what I was told to do, without asking questions, and certainly without ever negotiating over the details. On the contrary, you should negotiate - Everything.

What I learned, and want to pass on to you - Negotiate Everything in the workplace. You do not need to ask permission to negotiate. Be polite, be firm. You must also be very clear about what you are trying to accomplish, and about what your goals are. But you may negotiate, and do not need permission to do so.

You may negotiate pay, job responsibilities, due dates, and even to some extent who you are assigned to work with. I'm not encouraging you to be obnoxious about it, but for the things which are important, I'm encouraging you to negotiate.

Negotiate Everything, Including:

- Pay
- Job Responsibilities
- Job Assignments
- Due Dates
- Work Team

I am sure that there are plenty of things which I have not mentioned here. Those are negotiable too. Death and Taxes are also negotiable, to some extent - so do what you have to do, and Negotiate.

MARKETING, NETWORKING & SOCIAL MEDIA

Life Lessons Learned by Selling Girl Scout Cookies

During Girl Scout Cookie season of the 102nd anniversary of the Girl Scouts, I was helping to sell these delicious baked treats, And I thought about the lessons the girls learn every year while selling their cookies. It's more than just being able to earn badges... selling Girl Scout cookies actually teaches valuable life lessons that impact far beyond the here and now.

Girl Scouts teach important lessons about responsibility, business, networking, and life through the sale of the brightly-colored boxes of delicious cookies.

1. **BE FUN TO HAVE FUN.** As the band Harvey Danger says in their 1997 song, *Flagpole Sitta*, "If you're bored then you're boring," and this has stuck with me ever since. Easily one of the most difficult parts of the cookie season is having to sell outside a store for hours at a time trying to stop customers as they go in or out to buy a box (or 10) of cookies. It's fun at first, but after 3 hours or more, it gets pretty mind-numbing for the girls and for the parents. Some girls will complain they're bored, and my automatic response is, "If you're bored then you're boring"... and that's when I realized we need to exude fun to have fun. Once we started playing games, jumping around, singing and more, it helped pass the time, but it also grabbed people's attention. We sell way more cookies this way. This is an excellent lesson to learn for life and the workplace. People love and react to optimistic and fun people.

If you're dealing with a particularly difficult customer or client, try smiling. The results will likely be the same as a Girl Scout dancing while selling cookies in front of a grocery store – positive!

2. **NETWORK TO YOUR ADVANTAGE.** As times change, fewer girls are selling door to door due to safety concerns and many no-solicitation policies in neighborhoods. Instead, they have to use their networks – church friends, grandparents and their friends, friends, friends' parents, parents' friends and coworkers, and so on. Thinking beyond the immediate family and first line of best friends will help expand your network. Also, girls that make the most sales are the ones who carry their cookie sales sheets everywhere. They take them to school, sports events, church, volunteering, parents' workplaces, grandparents' workplaces, great-grandparents' nursing homes and more. To win the cookie selling game, the scouts must think outside the box (no pun intended) and not be shy about selling their cookies. This is the same as owning your own business or excelling at entrepreneurship. Creating and following through with a network is important, and you must put yourself out there without being afraid of being told "No!".

3. **LEARN TO ACCEPT NO'S.** Speaking of no's... while selling Girl Scout cookies, we discovered there are a huge number of people that don't like either Girl Scouts themselves or their amazing cookies ... how is that possible?! Also, many people don't carry cash (this is becoming more and more common), and others already ordered from their neighborhood scout. These discreet or straight "no's" are a disappointment, but the more the girls hear, the less they sting. While running a business, this is a difficult lesson to learn. The "no's" seem to always sting and can bring more frustration every time. No's are never fun, but with every no, adults need to take it the way these girls do – in stride. Don't let them get you down. Take a deep breath and move on to the next client. There is no sense in stressing over one "no" when there are potentially hundreds of "yes's" out there waiting for you!

While you're out buying your weight in Girl Scout cookies, remember, you're teaching these girls life and business lessons that will last their entire lives. Now, go buy those Samoas without an ounce of guilt!

Tips to Build Your Email List

A fairly advanced trick for business owners is to build your email list. If you want to take money to the bank, and grow your business aggressively, an email list is an absolute must.

Think of it this way – each time you send out an email, you're going to get requests for business. However, there are a few things that you need to know when building your email list and sending emails so that it works, and so that you don't get in hot water with the feds!

7 Important List Building Tips

1. Make sure that everyone you add to your list has given you explicit permission to add them to the list, or that they are a customer of record.

2. Every time you send out a communication, there must be a way to unsubscribe.

3. If you are going to send out emails, consistency is key! If customers know that they can expect a weekly email, or monthly email, then they will look for it. To get the best results, you have to be absolutely consistent about sending emails.

4. Deliver quality content to your list. Send helpful tips and advice that will have people interested in opening your emails.

5. Have a single call to action in each and every email. Tell clients what you'd like them to do, or ask them to do something. There needs to be a purpose behind the email, but don't ask them to do multiple things, or they will quite simply do nothing!

6. There is such a thing as sending too much email. You will burn out your subscribers quickly if you are too "spammy", or if you send out emails

too often. I've seen people recommend sending out daily emails, and segmenting the market aggressively. I'm not a fan of those techniques; they turn me off and make me click unsubscribe very quickly. If there is no value-add to the customer in your emails, they will quit reading!

7. You can build your list using Facebook, LinkedIn, your blog, and face to face contacts. Use all of your resources when building your email list.

One Thing You Should Not Do:

You should NOT add everyone you collect a business card from to your mailing list. It may seem tempting to do that, but it can get you into serious hot water with the FTC. Resist the urge to add everyone and anyone to your email list. It can cost you serious money in terms of fines and penalties. It can cause you to get booted from your email list management system. It will also cost you more. The truth is, you don't want to have a lot of people on your email list who will never buy from you or who aren't the appropriate target audience; you're going to be paying your list handler based on the size of your list. Don't do it! Just say no to adding everyone to your list.

CRM: What is it and How Do You Use It?

A very powerful tool for managing your business, almost any business, is a CRM, or Customer Relationship Management software. There are so many different CRM platforms out there, that it can make your head spin. Salesforce is one of the most ubiquitous ones, which is used across many different industries, but there are others like Savii, which is specific to the home care industry. Ontraport is very common in many industries, especially where there is a significant online portion of the sale.

What all of these systems have in common is a list of clients, and a list of their contact information. It also has a list of potential referral sources, so that you can track where your clients are coming from. This is important. You need to know who your clients are, and who sent them to you, or what you did specifically to acquire them.

From a client side, there is a tremendous amount that you can do. You can store information about client preferences, and use that later for data mining. If you are a travel agent, then you can list what kinds of travel a particular client is interested in, and you can even list which cruise lines, or travel companies that they prefer, so that when there are specials that match that particular client's interests, you can send information to that client. Say you have a client who prefers Disney Cruises and doesn't like Carnival. You can make sure you send them only Disney Cruise Line offers, and of course, other luxury travel options.

You can invent lots of ways to segment your client lists, and market specifically to clients based on their interests and preferences. It's also quite possible to market to your referral sources based on the referrals they've provided, and the type of information that the referral sources need to be successful.

In short, a CRM is a phenomenal tool for any company that does sales or has clients. Keeping track of how referrals are made, and the contact, and the effort that has been made, is important. It allows you to also draw out metrics, if you can ensure that the data is entered properly.

A good CRM will allow you to grow your business dramatically, and allow you to work on your business, instead of in your business. It's one of the most powerful tools you can use.

Drive Traffic to Your Website

Driving traffic to your website and getting in front of more people is the best way to raise visibility of your company, product or service. It's the holy grail for a lot of business owners - getting in front of more people to get more business.

To get more traffic, there are a few things you must do, and a few things that you may decide to do. Some are free, or inexpensive, and others are quite expensive. You need to decide how much that traffic onto your website is really worth, and whether there is a better way to do it.

So, without any more ado, here's how to drive that traffic to your website:

- **PUBLICIZE YOUR WEBSITE.** Make sure that you post links to your website from all of your social media accounts. That means that your Facebook profile needs to have your business listed. So does your LinkedIn profile.

- **CREATE A BLOG OR VLOG.** Content is king, and quality content is critical to getting website traffic. It's even better if you have engaging, quality content that has people coming back for more, because you speak their language and are solving their problems.

- Make sure you **UNDERSTAND THE AUDIENCE OF YOUR WEBSITE**, and fill a need or desire for them.

- **FIND YOUR PEOPLE** on Facebook, LinkedIn, Pinterest, Twitter, or other social media sites, and share content that you post with them. (But don't try to do every single social media platform out there!)

- **SUBMIT ARTICLES TO EZINE ARTICLES** to help drive traffic to your site. I have done it, and need to do more. It does indeed work!

- **SIGN UP FOR HARO**, or Help a Reporter Out, and respond to requests for information. Many of them will also quote you in the article.

- **GUEST BLOGS.** I have gotten great traction, and some amazing back links for this website with guest blogs that I've written for others. It needs to be unique content to benefit everyone, but I've found it is fantastic for driving traffic to your website!

- **VIDEOS ON YOUTUBE.** If you upload videos to Youtube, you can drive traffic back to your website. Make sure that they are high quality, and that they have proper tagging, and other information in them, so that you show yourself in the best possible light.

There are lots of things you can do to drive traffic to your website for free, but if you insist, there are lots of ways you can drive paid traffic to your website, including Google Adwords, Facebook Ads, Twitter Ads, and Pinterest Ads. Using these methods, you can drive as much traffic to your website, based on targeting, as you can stand. Another paid method, is Outbrain, where you pay to list articles, and they show up on a variety of websites, including the likes of CNN and others.

You! Quit Hiding!

I'm referring to you, me and almost every other woman out there. Like most female entrepreneurs, you are probably hiding your accomplishments from the world. Those of us who are guilty of this are masters of trying to hide our accomplishments and our businesses because we don't want anyone to think we're showing off. Because, you know, it's not lady-like to talk about our businesses and tell people about what we do. I'm entirely guilty of this on so many levels.

The reality is, many businesses fail, not because they suck, or are a lousy idea, but because nobody knows about them. Because we didn't do a good enough job telling the world about our business.

If a tree falls in the forest, and no-one hears it, does it make a sound?

When you start a business, you take on the responsibility of getting noticed, for the sake of the business, and so that your clients can find you. That means putting yourself out there rather than sitting down and shutting up. Your business and your family need for you to get yourself out there. You need to become visible to the rest of the world… and **Quit Hiding**.

That means taking some serious steps to become more visible. That means letting your family and friends know, and even calling them. It means getting out and going to Chamber of Commerce networking meetings. It means getting out from behind the desk, because the more time you spend out from behind the desk, the more well-known your business will be.

For my businesses, I've done a number of things to raise visibility, including a radio show, a book, blogging, Facebook Groups, Twitter, and going to Chamber of Commerce and other Networking meetings. Make a point of raising your visibility in the community and putting yourself out there.

You need to put yourself out there and be visible in the community to get the business you deserve. You need to become well known, and your business needs to become top of mind for the people in your community and target market. It's time to stop hiding and step out into the limelight.

Draw attention to yourself - in a good way - to build visibility for your business. You have to become essentially famous, business famous, and people have to know about you, like you and trust you. You need to do all this to get where you need to go and get the income you deserve to earn.

Quit hiding - so your business can grow and thrive!

Your Online Presence Can (and will) Sink You

Nowadays, if you own a business, chances are it is on the internet somewhere. People are mentioning it and sharing it on Facebook, or making comments about it on Yelp, or Google, or some other location online. Your online presence is crucial.

I can't tell you how many times, when I've been looking for information or a referral for a particular type of business, I start off by getting the contact information, and then go online to Google, and start searching.

The first thing I do is pull up the website, if I can find one, and the second thing I do is look at online reviews. If they don't have a website, with published contact information, I become instantly suspicious. If I find any bad reviews, I look to see how many bad reviews there are, then I move along to the next person or business if I see very many of those bad reviews.

Your website or Facebook page is critical here. If you provide a service, I want to see that others like you, and that there are pictures, if that's possible. I'd like to see before and after pictures, or other evidence of the work that you do. Not every business can or should give out information online about pricing, but I do believe that where it is appropriate, that information should be included. Also, your contact information should be everywhere on the web, and easily accessible. I prefer to see that you've registered with Google, and have posted your address, phone number, and an email address so that you can be contacted.

Pro Tip: Use a service like **Yext** to coordinate your address and phone number listings across multiple websites.

I get that a lot of business owners really don't care very much for Yelp or other similar review websites, because people can leave anonymous reviews. I get that these sites can be a double-edged sword, and they certainly can be impossible to manage and mitigate from a business owner's perspective. However, they can also be some of the most honest feedback you can get on a business. I figure where there's smoke, there's fire, and you can get a very good feeling on how a business is going to treat you if something goes wrong in those reviews. Obviously, I care that they do everything right the vast majority of the time, but what I really care about is what they do when things go wrong, because they can and will go wrong.

Notice I'm not suggesting that you should go online and set up accounts on Twitter, Pinterest, Instagram, Snapchat, Facebook, LinkedIn, and a Website on the first day you open your business. Some of those forms of social media can wait. Some of them, you may decide, don't really apply to your business. You do need to have some sort of appropriately professional presence online, and that is totally do-able without spending a fortune. If someone tells you that you need to spend thousands of dollars for a basic website, run the other way. There are other ways to set it up without spending huge dollar amounts. Be smart and be frugal. Don't spend all of your time online, because that's not how you make money. 'Likes' on Facebook don't equate to clients.

But you must have a solid, professional presence to attract the right kinds of customers.

Beware the Social Media Trap!

LinkedIn, Twitter, Facebook, Instagram, SnapChat, Pinterest... the list goes on. There are so many different social media platforms that it boggles the mind. It used to be that you could advertise on the TV or radio, and know that you were reaching most of your target audience. Nowadays, that's not true anymore, as more people have quit cable, and are instead on Hulu, Netflix, or hanging out on the internet on their computers, cell phones, or tablets. The market has segmented wildly, which means that it can be harder than ever to find your ideal clients. Don't fall into the Social Media Trap!

It's tempting to start opening accounts on all the different platforms, then creating a YouTube channel, an email list, a blog, and then try to maintain all of those as a startup company. Even if you had a dozen people working for you managing social media, it can be an incredible time sink, and you may not even be reaching your ideal clients on all the platforms because they may not even hang out there. Or, you may fail to respond to inquiries because you have so many points of contact that you lose business.

Neither scenario is particularly pleasant, so what is a business owner supposed to do? In short, you need to do a little bit of research, and think about who exactly your ideal client is, and figure out where they hang out online. Then you create an account in that place to reach them. For example, for Leadership Girl, my ideal client is a female over the age of about 25, who has job experience, and is in a leadership role, or is contemplating owning her own business. My ideal client for my Home Care business is actually the daughter of the client. She will typically be between the ages of 40 and 65, and likely will still have children at home, or recently graduated from college. In both cases, those ideal clients tend to hang out on Facebook and Pinterest. That's where I focus my time, and focus on engaging clients.

I make sure that where I'm spending my time is where that ideal client spends their time. I limit the amount of time I spend on Twitter, Pinterest, LinkedIn, Google Plus, and SnapChat. I'm pretty sure I'm not ever going to find a client on SnapChat, so I don't even have an account there.

In the words of one of my friends, time is money, so unless a particular platform is going to be bringing in clients, and thus money, don't bother with it. Don't try to open a gazillion accounts that you then have to monitor for activity. Don't do it. That way lies madness, and you won't have time to focus your time and energy on doing the things that matter the most to your business.

Subscribe to the KISS principle when it comes to social media. Focus on the ones likely to bring you revenue, and ignore the rest. You can't be everything to everyone, so it is not even worth trying.

The Real Life of Comments on Social Media

I've seen so many trolls and snarky comments online that I think I'm pretty immune to them at this point. Some people are seriously emboldened by their anonymity, and that makes them say things online and on social media that they would never, ever say to someone face to face. That can be a deadly mistake. Unfortunately, what most people don't realize is that once they post something online, it lives nearly forever. People can take screen captures of what has been posted, store those, and publicize them, but the websites themselves are legally bound to keep the data for a very, very long time.

So, a comment may be deleted, but it still exists in your user history. Think you can delete your user ID and have the information go away? Not so fast. That information is kept as well.

That stupid comment you made? Oh, it just stays around forever. The kid who told my daughter on Instagram, "If you post about my man again, and I'll gouge your eyes out"? Well, even though he regretted and deleted that comment, it isn't going to do him any good. We've got screen captures of it, showing it came from his userid. If it ever came down to a court case, then well, the police would simply subpoena the logs of what he's posted anywhere. Yes. That stupid comment you made as a teenager in the heat of the moment? It lives on forever. It can follow you forever. Threatening my daughter for posting a picture of an idol? Not so smart either.

Let me state that again. Comments you make online, send via text, email, or other electronic means, live on for a very long time. It doesn't matter if you delete those comments, because the records and logs of those are there, forever. It's a federal law. It also sucks. When I was a teenager, stupid stuff we said maybe ended up in a fist fight. Make a comment like that on social media, and you can land yourself in jail, with a record. There is no margin for error. For adults or for kids.

Watch what you say online. Treat it all as public, because it might as well be. Know that the stupid comment you make can and will live on forever. Oh, and I might decide to use you as an example in my blog.

TIME MANAGEMENT, PRIORITIES & GOALS

Pro Time Management

Pro time management is as much about what you do, as what you don't do. For me, pro time management revolves around a couple of simple concepts: Learning to get more done in less time, and remain sane. It's the gold standard for most parents and working adults. But how do you do it? I think that some of the time management skills can easily be taught, and are very simple. Maybe pro time management is too simple, but sometimes it can be difficult to follow.

Pro Time Management Concepts

- **TAKE CARE OF YOURSELF.** You can't expect to be productive if you don't give your body the rest, fuel or exercise it needs. It also means following up on nagging health problems and taking care of them. You wouldn't know it to look at me, but I actually exercise several days a week, and make a point of stretching, and doing other things to help with the exercise thing, despite the fact that I spend hours a day at the keyboard. (Cleaning bathrooms counts as exercise!) I give my body sleep, but I also make a point of taking time off from work, and unplugging entirely. Once, I went on a cruise with my family, and I did my usual hibernate for 4-5 days routine. I give my brain time to just turn "off" without reading, doing anything, or really thinking about much, other than to relax, and meditate, and spend time with my family. It is important that the down time be true down time, not just time playing on the computer, as that doesn't allow your body to get the same kind of deep rest.

- **FOCUS ON GETTING CERTAIN THINGS DONE AT TIMES OF THE DAY WHEN YOU'RE MOST PRODUCTIVE FOR THOSE TYPES OF THINGS.** I also make sure that I get stuff done during first shift which needs to be done during that time frame. For instance, I find that I write best first thing in the morning, and later in the evening. So, that's when I write performance appraisals, blog posts, and other things that require me to compose things. I have tried to listen to what my body and personality tell me, and focus on maximizing doing things when I'm most able to do them. That doesn't mean that occasionally I slog through things, it just means that I spend less time slogging and more time focusing on doing things when I'm most alert for that type of task.

- **SET UP A TO-DO LIST, BUT MAKE IT MANAGEABLE.** To-do lists are great things, in moderation. Knowing what you have to do and how much time it will take to do those items is key. Building a long to-do list with every task known to man is overwhelming, and chances are, you'll give up before you're done with the list, much less accomplishing everything on that list.

These are some of my top pro time management tips. What are your best time management tips? How do you balance things, and make sure that everything that needs to be done gets done?

Accomplish More Every Day With These Tricks

What would an extra hour or two every day do for your business? What would you be able to accomplish that you just aren't able to on a normal basis? Would you reach your weekly goals that you just can't seem to meet every week?

Here are some easy ways to gain time in 15-30 minute increments to help get more done. To figure out how much time you need to gain, figure out what you want to accomplish, then decide to spend the extra time to pursue it. After you commit this focus, then find where your time leaks.

- **DO MEAL PLANNING.** *Savings time: 20 minutes to 2 hours.* Instead of spending 20 minutes every afternoon dreading and trying to figure out what to make for dinner that evening, you can spend 10-20 minutes just one time per week planning out a weekly menu. When you go to the grocery store, figure out your whole weeks' worth of 3 meals and snacks so you only have to visit the grocery store once that week. You will stop having to worry about what's for dinner, and if plans change, it just gets moved to the next night. Simple!

- **DID YOU WASTE TIME IN TRAFFIC OR IN A WAITING ROOM?** *Savings time: 15 minutes to 1 hour.* If you find yourself waiting anywhere, in your car, in a doctors' office, then you should be listening to an educational podcast or book on CD or mp3. Even in 15 minute increments, you can learn a lot! Some have estimated that you can get a whole college degree worth of education just by listening in your car over the course of a couple years. In addition to educational listening and learning, you could do brainstorming, catch up on email, or write an email that you've been putting off. It's best to keep your tasks simple and convenient to carry so you can take advantage of these inevitable wait times.

- **GET READY FOR TOMORROW TODAY.** *Savings time: 30 minutes to 2 hours.* Check your last emails of the day, organize files, straighten up your desk, go through post-it notes, review to-dos, and get ready for the next day before your leave your desk or workspace for the day. By finishing one day and reviewing for the next you'll feel like one day's end is really complete and the next day is ready to start.

- **KEEP GOING AT QUITTING TIME!** *Savings time: 15 minutes to 1.5 hours.* Instead of flipping on Netflix as soon as the kids go to bed, use your pajama time and do just one more thing. Make sure it's just one simple task that doesn't need much energy, such as responding to emails or entering receipts for taxes. Do it now instead of tomorrow morning or putting it off until the weekend!

If you do all of these time saving tricks at once, then you could easily save 1-2 hours every day. What other tricks have you found to save yourself time each day?

Setting SMART Goals for Your Business

If you've set a goal and aren't specific about how you will achieve it… then it's just a wish, and likely to never be accomplished. The S.M.A.R.T. method is an acronym to help with setting and achieving goals in business: Specific, Measurable, attainable, Relevant, and Timely. It takes goals from blurry to real, actionable plans to achieve tangible and powerful results.

Here is the S.M.A.R.T method to goal setting for success:

- **SPECIFIC:** Your goal must be well defined. Vague goals are contrary to your goal because they don't offer adequate direction. Remember, you need goals to show you the way to success. You want to make it as easy as you can to get where you want to go by describing exactly where you want to wind up.

- **MEASURABLE:** Your goals should include specific amounts, dates, and so on so you can actually measure your success. If your goal is simply defined as, "To make more money", how will you know when you have been successful? In one month's time, if you have a 1% pay increase? Or in a year's time when you have a 100% increase? Without a way to measure your success, you will miss out on the excitement of knowing you have actually achieved your goal.

- **ATTAINABLE:** Make sure that it's possible to achieve the goals that you set. If you set a goal that you have no hope of achieving, you will only find yourself disheartened, and it'll kill your self-confidence. On the contrary, be sure not to set too-simple-to-reach goals. Setting realistic yet challenging goals, you will hit the balance you need. The goals you want are the ones that require you to "raise the bar"; they will bring the utmost personal satisfaction.

- **RELEVANT:** Goals should be relevant to the path you want your life and career to take. By keeping your goals aligned, you'll grow the focus you need to get ahead and do what you want.

- **TIMELY:** Your goals must have a deadline so you will know when you can celebrate your successes. When you are working on a time limit, your resolve increases and success will come that much quicker.

What part of the SMART method have you found works best for you?

Set Goals, Then Tell Others

One of the most powerful ways to set your direction is to begin with the end in mind. So, it is great to have goals, and know what you're working towards. But this is really part of a multi-step process. I would argue that you should set goals, then tell others. By sharing with others your plans, they become more concrete.

Have you ever thought, "I'm going to run a race"? Did you do anything about it? What happened when you set a goal and told someone about it? Telling others about my goals makes me feel more accountable to that goal. Sometimes it gives me the kick in the pants I need to do something. In my case, it's the nudge I need to actually get up and do my training for the half marathon I want to run next year. – Of course, now I've just told you about the goal. Do you think I'm more likely to get up and do my training now? I'd say it's likely.

Setting a goal is a powerful psychological tool. Telling people about that goal is yet another tool to add to your arsenal. It can't hurt to have lots of tools in your arsenal - and don't be afraid to use them.

What tools do you have in your bag to help you reach goals?

LEADERSHIP

I'm Not Your Mother

When I worked in corporate, there were a few co-workers who would refer to me as their den mother. That drove me crazy. In fact, unless I gave birth to you, I'm NOT your mother. I may be a mentor, or manager, supervisor, or leader. I may be many things, but please don't insult me by calling me a den mother.

I think that when we manage people, especially people who are entering the work force for the first time, they can require a lot of hands-on training. They require feedback and praise. Add in some generational dynamics about how different generations work, and the entire process can be quite time consuming, and occasionally draining. I spent a lot of time mentoring, getting people focusing on the right things, and helping kick start their careers. I focused on helping new hires establish habits that would enable them to be successful. Those habits included things like letting me know, and asking for more work, when they were running low on items to do, regularly sending status, and making sure that I knew what they were working on at all times.

I tried to teach a variety of different skills, like saying "no" when their plates were full, and sending status that conveys an appropriate amount of information to management.

This did not make me their mother. I do have four children of my own, but I'm really not in the business of signing up to adopt everyone that goes by. They're not orphans. They have parents of their own. It is a professional environment. To call me their mother demeans what I do, and the value that I add to the company.

So, please do call me mentor, manager, supervisor, boss, and possibly even awesome. Don't call me "mom" in a business setting unless I gave birth to you, okay?

How to Be an Effective Manager

Being an effective manager can be quite a minefield, but it doesn't have to be terribly tricky, if you throw yourself into it and follow some simple tips.

7 Tips To Be An Effective Manager

1. **BE GENUINE** – If you're fake, everyone is going to know it. You have to be genuine, and be yourself at a fundamental level. Represent yourself as you are, but that doesn't mean you have to volunteer too much info, just that what you volunteer is entirely your own.

2. **BE TRUTHFUL** – If someone asks you a question that you can't answer, just tell them that you can't answer. I'm not saying be hurtful or brutal, but that doesn't mean that what comes from your mouth has to be anything less than the absolute truth. If you can't change something, admit it. If you're not in control of a situation, acknowledge that as well.

3. **TAKE THE TIME TO GET TO KNOW YOUR EMPLOYEES** – This means knowing what their background is and where they want to go. Get to know their spouses' names, as well as their children's names, ages and hobbies. Most people will simply volunteer the information, if you listen. Then make a point of asking how things are going.

4. **UNDERSTAND YOUR EMPLOYEES' MOTIVATION** – Not everyone is motivated by the same things. Some people want money, others want title, public recognition, flexibility or a host of other things. It is impossible to use the correct carrot if you have no clue what it is.

5. **PRAISE PEOPLE EARLY AND OFTEN.** I can't say this enough. Praise, and thanks go a long way. Make sure that you are using these in about a 10:1 proportion with any negative or corrective actions.

6. **Do as you say** – If you can't walk the walk, then your employees won't either. Show up to work on time, and be fully present and engaged. Otherwise, you're giving them permission to do the same. While I was working on my MBA, I never, ever, not once, worked on school work at work, especially since I had 10 interns at the time.

7. **Don't play favorites** – This can be really hard, especially when you have someone who is a "problem child" reporting to you. I made a point of spending time with those prodigal children, so they knew I was watching, observing, and coaching them along. People notice when you play favorites, and it doesn't go over well. It breeds jealousy, and can be hurtful. At home, I refuse to tell my children whether I have a favorite child. Or I tell them that my favorite is the cat. The same applies at work, managing people.

Oh, and one last tip - Be Self Aware. If you don't know how you're doing, solicit feedback from your employees, and take corrective action if needed. It never hurts to do a '360', and see how things are going, and if they can be done better.

Being an effective manager isn't magical, and it doesn't happen by accident. Rather, it takes a lot of hard work, and diligence. Just like leadership, management is a skill that is learned, and is not necessarily innate.

7 Great Interview Questions

I can't take credit for all of my favorite interview questions, but I've used them over and over again in the last few years, as I've interviewed literally hundreds of candidates for various positions. Yes, there are the regular, run-of-the mill questions about a candidate's education, job history, and the like, but my truly favorite interview questions are those which really make the person stop and think. They give me a small window into how the person thinks, especially under pressure.

Here's my List of 7 Favorite Interview Questions:

1. **TELL ME ABOUT YOUR HOBBIES.** I'm particularly interested to hear about hobbies that someone is passionate about, even if they are unrelated to the current job. They show me that the candidate has some depth. I personally tend to pass on the people who tell me that they spend all of their time studying, and thus don't have any extra time to pursue any other hobbies. It makes me wonder how they will handle the myriad requests that we throw at our team, and the multitasking that is frequently expected.

2. **NAME 10 THINGS YOU CAN DO WITH A PENCIL THAT DON'T INCLUDE WRITING.** True story - I asked my own daughter this question, and the first 5 things she came up with involved destruction of some sort. But when we were able to get to well over 100 different items for this question at dinner one evening, it went up my list. Bonus points for a candidate if they come up with something we haven't thought of before.

3. **TELL ME ABOUT YOUR FAVORITE CLASS AND EXPLAIN WHY IT'S YOUR FAVORITE.** Honestly, if you can't answer this one (and are currently in school), I just pass over the resume. I frequently will get an answer of "I love all of my classes". In this case, you've failed to answer my question, and maybe are trying to deflect, but truly, I want to see how someone thinks, and this shows that they either are unwilling to play ball, or really don't have a clue.

4. **TELL ME ABOUT YOUR LEAST FAVORITE CLASS AND WHY IT'S YOUR LEAST FAVORITE.** This one goes along with the question above. I think I've always had favorite and least favorite classes, but I always had a reason.

5. **TELL ME ABOUT X ON YOUR RESUME.** If you say you speak a certain language, I may decide to interview you in that language. Let me just say that if you put it on your resume, it's fair game. Don't say I didn't warn you.

6. **WHAT DO YOU HOPE TO GAIN FROM THIS JOB?** This tells me that they've given some thought to the job for which they're applying, and why it might be a fit.

7. **WHAT THINGS DO YOU THINK WILL CHALLENGE YOU THE MOST IN THIS POSITION?** I don't ask them this question right off the bat, but if it's a second interview, this question is fair game. It is interesting to hear their thoughts

I've come across dozens and dozens of interesting interview questions. The number of interview questions is nearly limitless. Your creativity is the limit when it comes to interview questions, so take the time to figure out exactly what skills you are looking for in an employee and craft your questions around those skills and attributes.

Managing Personalities

Managing people is about managing personalities and conflicting interests. It's about figuring out what motivates people, and how to get them to do their jobs to your standards. It can be very hard. It is especially difficult getting people to do things that have to be done, but that don't particularly excite them.

Think about entering data into a database, or writing reports. Different people will approach the problem in distinctly different manners, but likely they will procrastinate, or prioritize other work over doing tedious tasks. So, how do you get them to understand the value of doing the mind-numbing tasks? Once they understand the value of those tasks, how in the world do you get them to actually DO them?

Every employee you meet, and indeed every person, is going to need and want different things out of their job, and out of their life. What this means is that motivating people and managing people is all about managing the individual personalities. I like to sit down and understand what is most important to each person. For some people, it will be a specific goal, such as going to Disney World. For others, a flexible work schedule is going to be a requirement. How many different motivators can you think of? Dozens off the top of your head, right? Money, Fame, Recognition, Time off, Travel, No Travel, Being able to spend time with kids, Flexibility, Regular bonuses, Flat salary. Each person has their own motivators, and the key is managing personalities and requirements.

Don't think that employees are going to change for you. They may give some, and approximate what you're trying to get them to do. Ultimately, though, you're going to have to bend yourself and conform yourself to their individual needs to be the most successful. So, look behind the mask, and figure out what motivates them, and where they want to go. Chart a path, and begin with the end in mind, because managing personalities is something that takes energy, time, thought, and some creativity at times. You may also decide that certain things you aren't going to deal with, and that's OK too. You need to decide what those are, and identify them clearly.

What about you? What do you think?

Simple Ways to Boost Employee Morale

Being a manager, supervisor, mentor, or team lead carries a lot of weight. You are responsible for making sure that your team gets work done, on time, with quality. Morale is something that feeds into this heavily. A happier team is generally more motivated to go the extra mile, and work just a little bit harder. Studies show that more money doesn't necessarily equate to more happiness among employees, so simply giving people raises isn't enough. As some of Dan Ariely's studies have shown, large amounts of money do not equal more performance, and may actually be inversely proportional. Don't get me wrong, money is good, and having enough of it is a requirement - because we all need enough to keep a roof over our head, food on the table, and a safe car to drive. So, enough money is a requirement. But it's not really a motivator.

So, what's a person to do? How do you get people to work harder, faster, better?

5 Tips to Boost Employee Morale

1. **GET TO KNOW YOUR EMPLOYEES.** Find out about their family's names, and ask how they're doing. I know about all of my Employees' significant others, and ask about them. I also make sure I keep up with what's going on in their lives.

2. **REMEMBER AND ACKNOWLEDGE MILESTONES.** If you do something as simple as having the team sign a card for a colleague who's getting married, having a baby, or whose wife has cancer, it means the world to them. It is not expensive, and cards can be had for .50 each at Dollar Tree. Show people that you care.

3. **TAKE THEM TO LUNCH ONCE A YEAR.** It doesn't have to be anything fancy, but my team really appreciates the one time per year that I take them out to lunch. Some of my former interns weasel themselves a lunch invite for that luncheon each year.

4. **GET THE TEAM TO ORGANIZE WEEKLY TEAM ICE-CREAM PARTIES.** In my office, Ice Cream Fridae, Wafters, and The Donut Club are all employee started, and run. You get on the signup list, and bring in ice cream every few months (or doughnuts, snacks, or some such). It means that the team gets together to socialize and blow off stress once a week. I've found that the weekly cadence is wonderful, because it's just often enough that people remember to bring in stuff, but not so often that we wear people out.

5. **EAT LUNCH WITH YOUR TEAM.** You can decide how much socializing you want to do, but make a point of eating lunch with the team every so often. The employees really appreciate the attention, and it's a good opportunity to build rapport.

So many simple ideas, so little time. Note that none of these take particularly large amounts of money. I do lots of little things, and could go on for days about the ideas - paper on the walls to color on, snacks in my office, and the yearly fish or treat party at Hallowe'en. Not a lot of money, but a huge morale booster for the entire group.

A Real Leader Builds the Next Generation of Leaders

I've heard it said that anyone can have followers, but a real leader builds the next generation of leaders. I think that is very true. It is not so difficult to get other people to follow you if you are smart and charismatic.

How do you build the next generation of leaders? What does it take? Can anyone be taught to be a leader? Or is Leadership an innate skill?

I think that leadership is a skill that is taught, and nurtured. Most people do not spring forth as leaders; many of the soft skills required take time, practice and maturity to develop. Likewise, it takes time and patience to nurture skills in other people. It takes a lot of patience to watch someone else do something that you likely could do yourself in half the time, and naturally do a better job at it. But by taking the time and energy to focus on creating a new generation, you yourself learn a lot. Many times you'll learn the subject better when you are the teacher. It is a great teaching trick: get someone to teach someone else, and suddenly they will have a much better mastery of the topic.

Think of Leadership in that sense. You yourself learn leadership skills by teaching them to others, and by building the next generation of leaders.

Lead By Example

I think that one of the most important things I can do as a female in a leadership position is to lead by example. I make a point of working with girls in Girl Scouts, and with boys in Cub Scouts. I try to mentor and lead young women, and to be a supportive role model. I want the next generation to understand that they have choices, and that they are privileged to make those choices.

I've heard it said before that you can't be what you can't see. If our sons and daughters never see women in leadership positions, then how will they ever visualize women in those positions? How much harder will it be for our daughters to have great opportunities if they don't see any women in those types of positions? To make matters worse, women are vastly outnumbered in STEM fields, and their numbers have been steadily dropping since peaking in the mid-1990's. Fewer and fewer girls are choosing to enter into engineering, computer science, and other related fields. The numbers are similarly dismal in other technical fields. How will we have enough qualified people to fill those jobs in this country if we don't encourage the next generation to follow in our steps?

I'll acknowledge that there is a tremendous amount of off-shoring going on. Frankly, there are only so many people in the world who do this type of work, anywhere, regardless of country, and as we develop new technologies, the need for more, qualified individuals will continue to grow. So, why not lead by example? Why not show our girls and boys that it is possible, and even desirable to have women in those careers?

I choose to take the opportunity to show young women that it is possible to have a family, be a Girl Scout Leader, and have a career. It is possible, but if you didn't see me do it, would you really believe it to be so?

Launching Others

A little while ago, I dropped my oldest daughter off at boarding school, and drove away, leaving her behind. I guess you could say, I launched my child. When we manage others, and bring them into a company, we are in a way, launching their careers.

5 Things to Keep in Mind When Launching Others

1. Give them the knowledge that they will need to be successful. At home, I have a lot of very frank discussions with my kids about how the world works. I do the same thing at work. I tell my employees who works well together, and who doesn't. I tell them in very concrete terms exactly what they need to know about a situation, and the pieces involved in it, because I want them to understand, not learn it the hard way.

2. Success is much more fun than failure. I set people up for success, not failure. If something isn't working, I tell them that. I also make sure to tell them when things ARE working as advertised.

3. Communicate, communicate, communicate. This one is key. Notice that the first two items above are about communication? When people come in from day 1, make sure that they understand, and know what the goals are, and communicate with them, early, often and regularly.

4. Make time for them. You can't get to know someone and understand their goals if you don't make time for them. Time is a requirement, not optional.

5. If you have the option of hiring someone, then hire someone better than you. I'm a firm believer that the company will be better off if I hire people who are always better than I am. And if I consider their

success to be a measure of my own. Likewise, I encourage them to hire people who they think are better than themselves.

I think it's important to realize that when you manage someone or have someone work for you, it probably isn't for life. You are in this part of their life for this time period for a reason. They will eventually move on to the next phase of their lives, and it may be sooner, or it may be later, but it is only a phase. What you are doing now will lead to that next phase, and if you can keep that in mind when managing people, and allow them to launch and fly away at the right time, it will be a win-win.

Lead Yourself

It's always easier to tell someone else to change than to take an uncomfortable moment to look at your own actions. Real leaders embrace those uncomfortable moments as opportunities to get to know themselves better.

A core element of leadership is to be self-aware – that is to know your strengths, weaknesses, blind spots, and areas that you'd like to continue to develop. An effective leader knows she can't do it all, and has the confidence to delegate and ask for support. She also builds a team that compliments her weaknesses and is empowered to tell it to her straight when they think she is leading them down the wrong path.

Here are some questions/ideas that will help you get to know yourself better:

- What would you be doing if no one was looking?
- What do you not enjoy doing and have to do? Is this a work flow issue that can be delegated to someone more suited to the task?
- Ask others what they think your strengths and weaknesses are and compare their answers with your answers. Do an honest assessment.
- Test your limits by participating in activities you normally wouldn't do.
- Set yourself some stretch goals. These are goals that go slightly above your current skill level. See what kind of insights and experiences you gain from them.

- Take time for yourself to be with yourself. Drink tea alone in a shop. Sit in a quiet place to contemplate. Keep a journal. Learn to keep yourself company.

Your business and career will do infinitely better if you learn to be self-aware. I'm not saying that you are necessarily going to ever have a perfect view of how others see you, but if you will take the time to look in the mirror, and listen carefully to what others are telling you, you will do infinitely better. No person on the face of this earth is perfect, and no person is completely evil. Some people do, however, lack the self-awareness to see when they are wrong, and correct their path.

CLOSING

Are You A Believer?

Do you believe in what you're doing? Do you believe in your career? In your business? If the answer is "yes", then great! If the answer is "no", then we need to have a serious heart to heart. Seriously, talk to yourself. In a quiet room, think about what you're doing, and ask yourself if you believe in it. Do you do it well? Is it something you are passionate about? Let's be honest. Working a job that you aren't passionate about is just a job. If you dislike it, then it can be a soul-sucking, joy-robbing pain. Is that how you want to live your life?

Doing something that you believe in and that fulfills you is important, because it makes it so much easier to get out of bed in the morning. It is also much more likely that you'll put a lot more effort into the job, and focus on doing that job well. That in turn translates to improved performance, and better results. I've felt that lift in my soul when I like what I'm doing, and I've also felt that darkness each day, as my soul dies a bit, when I haven't liked my job nearly as much.

What if you're only "so-so" about the job? Well, that means that you're less likely to go the extra mile on it. You're also not going to get as much out of it, or focus on being your best at the job. You're not going to be able to solve problems or function nearly as well if you're working in a job that is a poor fit. I've lived it, and been in those jobs where I suffered from analysis paralysis. "Am I going to get in trouble for this? Or this?" Worse yet is that feeling of losing your soul to something that you don't really believe in, and really don't even enjoy doing.

Why would you spend your life doing something you don't particularly care for or believe in, if you have a choice? Believe it or not, we all have choices. Make the choice to step away, and find something else that is a better fit. What I found when I switched jobs was that I suddenly was better able to spend endless hours devoted to my job. I could lay my head down at night, content with what I'd done that day.

Can you say the same for your job/career? Why don't you try changing it? What's stopping you from making a change, and becoming a believer in what you do?

****

THE END

You can find me online at LeadershipGirl.com